PRASE FOR
Too Safe for Their Own Good:
How Risk and Responsibility Help Teens Thrive

At a time of escalating anxiety about teenagers, *Too Safe for Their Own Good* is the wake-up call we've been waiting for. Ungar not only shows why too much safety and not enough risk is a bad thing for adolescents, but he also gives practical tips for finding the right balance. Written with both authority and a light touch, this is required reading for parents, educators and anyone else who cares about our teens.

—Carl Honoré, author of
In Praise of Slow and Under Pressure

Too Safe for Their Own Good offers us fresh, powerful and deeply relevant ideas about the developmental needs of teenagers. Ungar's thought-provoking book is both wise and practical. All of us parents, therapists and educators who work with adolescents will benefit from his ideas on what teenagers require for optimal growth. This is a paradigm-shifting book.

—Mary Pipher, Ph.D., author of *Reviving Ophelia*

Michael Ungar clearly demonstrates that risk and responsibility are meat and potatoes for the teenage soul; and he delivers his message to parents with compassion and the hard-earned wisdom of a veteran practitioner.

—Chris Mercogliano, author of *In Defense of Childhood: Protecting Kids' Inner Wildness*

Too Safe for Their Own Good is a terrific book. It offers parents such a different and smart view of raising teens that every parent should read it.

—Evan Imber-Black, Ph.D., author of *The Secret Life of Families* and director of the Center for Families and Health, Ackerman Institute for the Family

Michael Ungar has written an exciting, timely, and important book, one that significantly advances understanding of the bases of resilience and health among diverse children around the globe. He provides an innovative and insightful conception of the central role that both risk and responsibility play in enabling young people to thrive and to become adults who are ready to contribute to families, communities, and civil society. The vision and voice in this book compellingly illustrate why the scholarship of Professor Ungar is regarded internationally as a vital resource for enhancing science, policies, and programs fostering well-being among young people everywhere.

—Richard Lerner, Ph.D., author of *The Good T*

Author, social worker and family therapist Michael Ungar's experience shows us the unintentional harm that can come from good intentions. . . . Ungar helps us understand that over-parenting and trying to reduce the risk of physical harm to zero leads to unintentional side effects. . . . Let's take off the bubble wrap and let our kids breathe.

—Silken Laumann,
Olympian and author of *Right to Play*

This book is a must-read for all parents who worry about their children's safety and wellbeing. Michael Ungar, an internationally respected expert on raising resilient youth, provides valuable information and vivid case illustrations in this practical resource. In today's hyper-stressed and precarious world, families more than ever need his research-informed wisdom and guidelines to help their children avoid harmful risks and yet actively engage life challenges to build resilience and encourage positive growth.

—Froma Walsh, Ph.D.,
author of *Strengthening Family Resilience*

This book will be of great interest to parents and practitioners. Especially useful is the guidance Ungar provides about how to empathize and understand the function of risky behavior on the road to helping children grow and thrive. The title emphasizes a central message of the book, i.e., "Do not 'protect' children from opportunities to engage in challenging experiences," but the scope of the book is much broader, addressing many important questions faced by today's youth and their families.

—Barbara Friesen, Director, Research and
Training Center on Family Support and
Children's Mental Health, Portland State University

With *Too Safe for Their Own Good*, Michael Ungar is likely to touch the parent of any teenager. He illustrates the positives of what many see as only negative: taking a risk. What child learned to walk without daring to take that first step? What teen learned to drive without turning the key for the first time? Risk is essential for children to develop, and Ungar kindly instructs parents how to help their children discover the right balance between taking risks for growth and taking risks to the point of harm. This book is a must-read for parents worried about their risk-taking youth.

—David C. Schwebel, Ph.D., Associate Professor and Vice
Chair, Department of Psychology; Director, UAB Youth
Safety Lab, University of Alabama at Birmingham

the we generation

the **we** generation

RAISING SOCIALLY RESPONSIBLE KIDS

MICHAEL UNGAR

Da Capo
LIFE
LONG

A Member of the Perseus Books Group

Designed by Brent Wilcox
Set in 11 point Sabon by the Perseus Books Group

Library of Congress Cataloging-in-Publication Data

Ungar, Michael, 1963–
  The we generation : raising socially responsible kids / Michael Ungar.—1st Da Capo Press ed.
    p. cm.
  Includes bibliographical references and index.
  ISBN 978-0-7382-1378-1 (alk. paper)
  1. Parenting. 2. Youth—Conduct of life. 3. Compassion. 4. Social values.
I. Title.
  HQ755.8.U56 2009
  649'.7—dc22
                                                              2009026194

First Da Capo Press edition 2009

Published by Da Capo Press
A Member of the Perseus Books Group
www.dacapopress.com

Da Capo Press books are available at special discounts for bulk purchases in the U.S. by corporations, institutions, and other organizations. For more information, please contact the Special Markets Department at the Perseus Books Group, 2300 Chestnut Street, Suite 200, Philadelphia, PA, 19103, or call (800) 810-4145, ext. 5000, or e-mail special.markets@perseusbooks.com.

10 9 8 7 6 5 4 3 2 1

If you want to be miserable, think about yourself.
If you want to be happy, think of others.

SAKYONG MIPHAM RINPOCHE

CONTENTS

AUTHOR'S NOTE
The Children and Their Families

In order to protect the privacy of all the individuals with whom I have had the privilege to work, the stories I share in this book are a blend of both real, but disguised, and imagined details and are based on the lived experience of the many young people and their families that I have met through my research and clinical practice. The youth and their families in these pages are substitutes for, or composites of, individuals whose identities must, of course, remain confidential. None of the people portrayed actually exist as I describe them. If some readers think they recognize someone in these pages, the resemblance is purely coincidental. Perhaps, if the stories sound familiar, it is because throughout my career in a number of communities, big and small, I have met hundreds of young people and families with much in common.

PREFACE

I started writing this book on the day the principal of our local elementary school told me about a conversation he'd had with a parent of one of his eleven-year-old students. Driving home after work, he'd passed the boy, who was playing road hockey with his friends. When the principal waved hello, the boy shouted back, "F——you!" and then, with a big smirk, went back to his game. The next morning, with a defiant boy in his office, the principal phoned the boy's mother. He was astounded when she told him, "You have no right to discipline my son. He was off school property and it was after school hours. You have no say over what he does. I'll decide what to do with him, not you."

The principal stammered, "I see," and hung up. He still gave the student a detention, but he wondered later what would become of such a boy.

I wasn't that surprised by the mother's response. I've seen fathers at my children's soccer games yell insults at thirteen-year-olds on opposing teams. I've seen parents at the university where I teach hire lawyers to defend their sons and daughters who have been caught plagiarizing. I've seen a mother of a three-year-old complain angrily to a day-care worker that another three-year-old was bullying her child by not getting off the playground swing quickly enough.

While parents don't consciously raise their children to be self-centered, there are subtle and not-so-subtle things we do that teach our children to think about themselves ("me") first, and about others and their own connection to those others ("we") second. We can decide to consciously steer our children in the direction of more socially responsible behavior. I'm convinced their generation has the potential to become far more connected with others and more compassionate than the generation raising them was raised to be (that's us). In the pages that follow, I'll show how to raise children to think *We* during these *Me*-thinking times.

Online but in Need of Touch

Say the phrase "connected kids," and most parents think about an Internet generation of MSN-chatting, online-gaming, text-messaging, and YouTube-surfing young people. They think of children sequestered in their bedrooms, surrounded by technology, hardly wanting to break for dinner. This book is about a different kind of connected child.

Despite appearances to the contrary, our kids still crave old-fashioned flesh-and-blood connections with their parents and with lots of other adults in their communities besides. Children need to feel close to those who populate the "village" that raises them. But our children, whether they are five years old or fifteen, need parents the most.

One parent or two, stepparents, or a caring grandparent who takes over when necessary—it doesn't really matter who's doing the parenting as long as it includes modeling the compassion that nurtures children's own caring instincts.

When we show children compassion, the odds are that they will grow up giving a damn about others and caring about people in their families and communities as much as they care about themselves. They'll become a We Generation.

Raising children to think "We" might just help us rethink some of our own Me-thinking ways. After all, many of us grew up in Me-thinking times. We feel guilty about driving huge gas-guzzling vehicles, but keep driving them to get our children safely to school or hockey practice. We try to forget the impact our actions have on the environment, while our children in the backseat report what their teacher said about global warming and our environmental footprint. We don't mean to segregate our communities, but we choose to live in gated communities just the same. We blush with embarrassment when our children finally notice that the poor people have been pushed away. We mumble something about "That's just the way it is," or make a donation to the food bank, but we are shy to say anything about how our choices are part of the problem. We want our children to have access to every available medical and social service imaginable, but we look for ways to avoid paying our taxes, hoping someone else will foot the bill. We don't mean to be so self-centered, but as individual adults, we haven't shown much inclination to take responsibility for the fiscal, environmental, or social liabilities we are leaving our children. It is a small step from such selfishness to the actions of the parent who excuses her son's belligerent behavior when his principal calls home.

An Overview of the Book

Each chapter that follows provides part of the solution to the problem of self-centered kids. At the end of each chapter, you'll also find a Tips List that shares suggestions from parents regarding how to help your children perform everyday acts of kindness.

The introduction begins with setting out what I mean by a We Generation. It talks about what our children really want (connections) and how parents can nurture We-thinking by showing kids what it means to act compassionately toward others. Through stories about young people who want connections with their parents, I demonstrate the pivotal role parents play in preparing the We Generation for its contribution.

In Chapter 1, I show that lots of parents are already doing many things right when it comes to raising We-thinking kids. In this chapter, readers are provided an exercise to reflect on their successes and then are given information on the stages children and youth grow through as they become moral beings capable of giving back to their families and communities.

Chapter 2 explores the importance of attachments to others in the lives of children. It shows how interactions with adults begin a cycle of growth. Compassion leads to connections, then to responsibility, and finally to citizenship. An exercise helps parents evaluate how much their child is thinking We already. The chapter also discusses the dangers our children face when they and their parents fail to adequately connect: selfishness, alienation, exploitation, and disenfranchisement.

Chapter 3 stresses the importance of connections to other adults besides parents. Grandparents, neighbors, and the parents of our children's friends can all help children learn to think We. I also take a look at what divorce means to children's sense of connectedness and how we can help them feel attached even when their parents are in conflict and nuclear families splinter.

Chapter 4 looks critically at why we have stopped touching our children. Through lessons learned around the world, I challenge readers to let their children be touched physically by the adults in their lives. With appropriate touch, children learn to show compassion for others.

In Chapter 5, I discuss the value of both emotional and spiritual connections for children. I show how children substitute sexual activity for emotional intimacy. I suggest ways parents can become their children's spiritual and emotional guides. But this chapter also emphasizes that raising a We Generation doesn't mean telling children how to express themselves or what to believe; we help children best when we help them show tolerance for others.

In Chapter 6, I show how we can invite children of any age to take responsibility for themselves and others. To make these invitations, we need to speak with children in ways that draw them into their families and communities. In this chapter, I help parents find ways to have engaging conversations with their children.

Chapter 7 makes the argument that those large "monster" homes in brand-new suburbs can put children at risk. This chapter takes a critical look at how we have built our communities and our houses. It argues that many of the structures we have built fail to help children connect with their parents or with their communities. It suggests solutions as well, ways we can fight against the anonymity children experience in big houses in wealthy suburbs.

In Chapter 8, the focus shifts from our children's homes to their "villages." It's all well and good to say it takes a village to raise a child, but how exactly do we get our children to think about the welfare of all villagers? In this chapter, I offer examples of how young people can be inspired to think about their community and, even more importantly, how communities can make themselves inviting for young people. From the work of Jane Jacobs to the thoughts of Marc and Craig Kielburger, this chapter provides practical ideas to make villages kid-friendly places.

The Conclusion shows that children who experience compassion at home and in their communities are at an advantage globally. These are the young people who will have the emotional and moral foundation from which to navigate cyberspace safely. Realizing the potential of a We Generation, however, depends on how well our children experience compassion, are provided responsibility, and engage as citizens.

Beyond Me-Thinking

Finding solutions to Me-thinking ways requires that we ask ourselves several questions:

- What can we do as parents to help young people think We instead of Me? Our children today need (and want) guidance from parents if they are to realize their potential as a We Generation.
- How can we build our homes, communities, and schools so that young people feel connected? The structures we provide make a difference. Children are more likely to think We when provided homes, communities, and schools that make connections easier.
- How can we protect our children from such dangers as Internet predators, the glorification of violence, or the emotional crush of busy families and unconnected com-

munities? The compassion we show our children in our homes can inoculate them against the dangers they face beyond our front doors.

There is a saying about wealth: The first generation earns it, the second generation saves it, and the third spends it. My hope is that our children do not ignore the sacrifices their grandparents and great-grandparents made with their lives to ensure peace and security. These elders were the forebears of the We Generation. In fact, studies show that today's children resemble their grandparents more than they do their parents when it comes to their behavior in social spaces.[1]

Regardless of who our children mimic, if we teach young people compassion and insist that they share responsibility for others, the legacy of past generations won't be wasted. This is a time of opportunity, of the (post)modern family.

introduction

The We Generation

On the streets of a city that is just big enough to have city-sized problems, a group of girls hang out in a downtown square. Many come from good homes. Hanging out on the street is an easy way to find adventure. They have tattoos on their backs and shoulders and piercings in their tongues and eyebrows. Their hair has streaks of red and magenta. They use the f-word without apology and brag about sex. They smoke pot. They want to fight. They like the way the couples strolling through the square on warm summer evenings stare at them, then quickly move on. The girls know people are on edge when they're around.

The girls will all eventually go home. Christina will slip through the back door of her 2,700-square-foot palace, with surround-sound televisions and four bathrooms, one for each family member. She will call out a halfhearted "I'm home" to her parents, who went to bed hours earlier. Perhaps one of them will wake up long enough to come downstairs and tell her, "Good night, now," before heading back to bed, and that will be Christina's cue to wander into the kitchen and find a plate of leftovers in the fridge from the dinner she missed. She'll eat by herself at the kitchen island. Still slightly stoned on the weed the girls were given by the men they teased, she won't bother to reheat the plate but will just nibble a bit on the pork chop, tough and overdone from waiting for her. The quiet makes her feel sad. She gives her old dog a pat, then climbs the stairs.

She feels so alone. She wants to talk to someone, but the people who matter most are the ones she's pushed away. Her relationship with her parents is a tangled mess of demands and gnashing of teeth. As she passes their room, she thinks about going in, waking them up, sitting between them, talking about the rude things she heard, feeling safe and perfect again. Instead, she goes to her room and locks the door behind her. She stretches out on her bed, the room spinning from the effects of the pot she smoked, and she strains to hear the muffled snores of her father in the next room and murmurs from her mother, who lies next to him.

Lying on her bed, Christina closes her eyes and thinks back to the social worker who visited the girls on the street tonight. She was in her thirties. With jeans that had no rips. And a jacket, black, with a white crest that told everyone the name of the organization she works for. She passed out condoms. And pamphlets about safe sex. And asked the girls if they needed anything. Christina liked the social worker. She'd seen her there before. She was helping the girls tell City Council why they needed the square. Why they didn't like the police chasing them away. Why the city should put in public toilets for them to use at night.

Christina rolls on her side to slow down the room's spinning. She recalls that the woman asked the girls what they would do if they got pregnant. Christina had shouted, "I'd keep it! Raise it!"

"So, what would you do if your own daughter ran away from home?" the social worker asked. "Was living on the street, here on the square most nights?"

Christina had drawn hard on the joint she was holding. The smoke curled into her eyes, so that they teared up a little. She squinted at the social worker. "If she ran, I'd go find her. There is absolutely nothing that could stop me from going and looking for her. F——in' nothing." The girls all nodded. They like it when Christina gives them a voice, says what they're thinking. "And if I found her, I'd haul her back home."

"I believe you, Christina," the social worker said. "Are you telling me, though, that if your own mother came and found you now, that you'd go home with her?"

Christina laughed. "Hell, no," she said. Then she stared at the social worker, her eyes still moist. "But I'd want to be found."

Lying there in the dark, Christina's thoughts drift to the street. Then back to the emptiness she feels at home and the argument she can expect over breakfast the next morning. As she finally passes out, the room lurching around her, she mouths quietly to herself, "Who cares . . . who . . . f——in' . . . cares."

The We Generation

At this time of great social change and technological innovation, it's easy for parents to overlook what kids really want:

connections. Not electronic, virtual, real-time chatter, but one-on-one attention and touch. All our computer-driven mass communication is creating a generation that can gossip at lightning speed, research anything about anyone with a few keystrokes, and morph into uncontrolled communities in cyberspace. This generation is more connected than any other before it, but the connections are superficial. Beneath the whirling cacophony of the information revolution are children pleading for someone to notice them. They are looking for genuine connections with concerned adults: parents, teachers, coaches, even the store clerk who sells them a Red Bull. Our children want to be known to others. They want their parents to notice them. They want to be loved and caressed. And they want to be held responsible, for themselves and for others.

If we don't believe it, it's because we have chosen to believe instead the stories about young people we hear in the media, movies, and advertising—stories that just aren't true. While it may not always seem so, they are not all troubled kids. Growing up needn't be a time of "storm and stress."[1] Despite a few blowups that end in "I hate you," our children want to play a part in their families and communities, at least they do when they are given the opportunity.

The We Generation is a reaction to the individualism we've handed them. As sociologist Zygmunt Bauman tells us, we are in a time of "liquid modernity."[2] Everything we assumed was solid is in flux: identity, community, geographic boundaries, loyalties. Our children live in a time when they have far more choice than did any other generation at any time in history. Their connectivity through the Internet and a five-hundred-channel universe means they can pick and choose bits of their identity from around the world. Our children's music can be world beat–infused Indian hip-hop, retro

1960s rock, electric pop, or Colombian salsa. Kids can wear their hair long and shaggy like their favorite rock star or weave it into dreadlocks or dye it green for something radically different. They have, superficially, endless possibilities, in a world that floods them with one identity choice after another. Their allegiances to any one movement, belief, or community are serial. They thrive on temporary monogamy, choosing to forget that change is inevitable.

The paradox, however, is that with this freedom to migrate between identities comes a profound wish for belonging. Capturing this push-pull tension between individualism and belonging, Swedish management consultant and futurist Mats Lindgren calls this generation of young people born since the late 1980s the MeWe Generation. From his research with young people in Europe since 1989, Lindgren has found that the more one is individualistic, the less one feels whole: "Although the MeWes travel and experience more than any other generation before them, the small things in life still get the highest scores. A happy life is based on relations and companionship."[3]

While Lindgren paints a picture of young people balanced between the Me-thinking of their parents' generation and the We-thinking that is possible today, I believe that kids crave opportunities to think We more often than to think Me.

They're lonely out there on their own. Like Christina, they want to find a place where they belong. They want their "herd." The breadth of their individual options makes it more important than ever that they commit to relationships, identities, and values that define them. Without belonging somewhere, they risk becoming nameless and lost.

When I've met young people in my clinical practice or in our juvenile detention centers, schools, and mental health facilities and asked them what they need, they tell me over and over again the same thing:

- *Roots:* Our children need to know that their lives have a past, present, and future. They want to know where they came from so that they can understand where they are going.
- *Wings:* The freedom to travel (whether with one's body or one's mind) is an empty promise without the security of knowing that no matter how far one roams, there is a place to come back to where the world makes sense.
- *Audience:* What good are all those individual expressions of personality if no one is there to notice or applaud our choices?
- *Compassion:* Our children need others to show them that their thoughts and feelings count.

If there is a Me Generation, then it's to be found among us, the baby boomers and their children who are today's parents. Fed on an explosive mix of sexual liberation, challenges to church and state, resistance to war, and rampant consumerism, we have run up national debts, built impractical and environmentally unsustainable suburbs, worked liked demons, ignored our families, obsessed over security rather than philanthropy, and generally lived by the rule "What's good for me is good." It's tough to look in the mirror and admit that we haven't been the best role models for our children.

This next generation is trying to be more balanced. Their slogan might well be, to borrow a phrase from Alexandre Dumas's *Three Musketeers,* "All for one, and one for all." They are individuals who want commitments.

Children of the We Generation are opting out of careers that undermine the balance between time at work and time in relationships. They are choosing to focus elsewhere than on their survival. The social safety net means they aren't anxious about their futures. Nor are they obsessing on success, either, much to their parents' dismay.

This We Generation is guided by a new set of principles:

- The We Generation understands that its capacity to connect to others is limitless. Children of the We Generation say to themselves, "I can have many friends," "I can buy whatever I want whenever I want it, if I have the resources," and "There will always be someone in another time zone who wants to play."
- Children of the We Generation understand that the world is a very small place and that their actions affect others. A flu bug in my community can infect yours; a shooting ten thousand miles away will likely be the dinner conversation in my home, just as it is in the homes of the victims' neighbors.
- The We Generation understands that our connections with others are many and complex. There is a good chance that someone I know knows someone who knows you.
- Children of the We Generation understand that they have a responsibility to others in their families, their communities, and beyond. Mutual assured survival depends on it.

Offer this generation the roots, wings, audience, and compassion it needs, and its children will show themselves to be great joiners and social planners.

Our Role As Parents

Despite our own hyperindividualism, it's within our power as parents to raise a generation of We-thinking kids. In the chapters that follow, I'll show that three aspects of our relationships with our children encourage them to become a part of the We Generation:

1. *Showing compassion:* We help our children to forge strong bonds with us by showing them they matter. The child who is shown compassion when she expresses her thoughts and feelings (being listened to is always more appreciated than a mini-lecture) is more likely to extend the same compassion to others.

2. *Modeling beneficence:* When we model how to give our time and energy to others in our families and communities, we develop in our children a sense of morality and philanthropy (when we volunteer, our children are more likely to follow our example).

3. *Inviting responsibility:* When we expect our children to make a contribution to the welfare of their families (even walking the dog is appreciated) and communities (a little help fund-raising goes a long way) and hold them accountable for their actions, we convey to them that they have a purpose and place where they belong.

Consider what happens when we don't teach our children about compassion, beneficence, and responsibility. In such a climate, they are raised to think Me instead of We. As their parents, we risk their futures when we follow these Me-thinking behaviors:

1. *Promote individualism:* When we overemphasize self-protection, individuation, and prejudice toward others, we teach our children to think about themselves rather than

their part in a weave of relationships and mutual dependency. (How often do we host exchange students in our home or take in cultural festivals that help our children understand the lived experience of others?)

2. *Model privilege:* When we make our children feel entitled, or model how to exercise their rights without showing them how to contribute, we teach them to take without giving back. (What opportunities exist in your community to teach your child responsibility for those less fortunate?)

3. *Excuse irresponsibility:* When we stop expecting our children to give of themselves and defend them when they exercise bad judgment, we make them into overprotected babies who never grow up. (How often does your child have to suffer the consequences of his actions and admit when he has done something wrong?)

We promote Me-thinking among our kids through what we do, what we say, and how we shape our children's physical and social worlds. Unfortunately for young people like Christina, we are raising many of them in middle-class mansions in vast suburbs with few places to connect to one another (I'll talk more about this in Chapter 7). The world Christina lives in squashes connections. We've stopped letting our children walk to school, ride public buses, or go to the park in small groups without an adult to supervise them. Though we protect our children from the consequences of their actions, we still expect them to take responsibility for themselves, their families, and their communities. Through our words and deeds, we demonstrate how to act selfishly.

I fear that we are raising a generation that resembles more the Me Generation of its parents than the We-thinking ways of our children's grandparents and great-grandparents.

If we want children to think We, then we will have to model for them the compassion that seeds a sense of collective responsibility. Sixty years ago, our elders showed themselves to be We-thinkers when called to a just and necessary war. Our children desire an equally powerful purpose.

Where Compassion Shows, a We Generation Grows

What is compassion? Think back to when you were a child and you stared at the bruised knee and fretful tears of a friend and began to cry, too. Or you wondered how another child felt when she appeared hungry or sad. Compassion is our experience of attunement with another's suffering. It is also our desire to alleviate that suffering, to acknowledge "I can help." When feelings meet action, there is a spirited moment of connection in which my well-being and another's are intertwined. At that moment, compassion and action are inextricably linked. I must help, if only because I can.

Compassion is the stone from which we sculpt a We Generation. The phrase *We Generation* has been bandied about by many, but the one who epitomizes its meaning best is a young man named Craig Kielburger.[4] A child rights advocate for the past dozen years, Kielburger was only a child himself when he began to address issues of children's rights. His efforts have brought him and the Free the Children organization he founded in 1995 a host of awards, including the World's Children Prize for his efforts advancing the rights of children. His awareness of what needed to be done began at age twelve, when he learned of the murder of Iqbal Masih, a child laborer in Pakistan who was the same age as Craig. It was the spark that turned a privileged North American youth with a social conscience into a human rights activist. Free the

Children now helps educate tens of thousands of children internationally. On the home front, Kielburger is also the co-founder of Leaders Today, an organization that sends speakers into schools to promote and inspire positive social change and citizenship.

Of course, Kielburger didn't just arrive at that level of consciousness without some help. In his writing and public appearances, he acknowledges that his parents and older brother have played a big part in his success. They nurtured in him something special. It's not far-fetched to say that most great children's achievements that make the world a better place are at least partly inspired by their parents. Our children follow our lead, whether our efforts are quiet and un-obtrusive, or magnanimous and newsworthy. Retired stock brokers and businesspeople routinely make sizable contributions to charities, often anonymously. A stay-at-home mother offers a helping hand to an elderly neighbor recuperating from a fall. Warren Buffett donates billions to the Bill & Melinda Gates Foundation, creating a philanthropic powerhouse of unimagined proportions. The father of my daughter's best friend is the enthusiastic coach of my daughter's soccer team. My own family makes space for exchange students in our home. While the work accomplished through such acts of kindness, big and small, is important, no less important is the lesson these donations of one's time and money teach our children about compassion for others.

Far from being a generation of troubled children and teens, today's young people are great contributors to their communities. In fact, a 2008 survey of 60,000 American households by the Bureau of Labor Statistics of the U.S. Department of Labor found that among youth aged sixteen to nineteen, 25.9 percent volunteered through or for an organization at least once in the previous year.⁵ On average, they gave forty hours of their time to recreation organizations, fund-raising efforts, and other community activities. Though the adults around them aged thirty-five to forty-four are more likely to volunteer (31.3 percent report volunteering) and for more hours, youth give of their time through many informal efforts that benefit family and neighbors just as often as these actions benefit organizations.

We can see young people's efforts to give of themselves gaining momentum, in part because the Internet has made it possible to mobilize youth like never before. Youth Service Day, an event sponsored by the State Farm Companies Foundation, is a national and global celebration of youth contributions. Reaching out to more than 60 million people worldwide, the event provides young people with an opportunity to tutor children, engage in disaster relief, register voters, educate communities on issues such as nutrition and sexual health, and, in any number of other ways, make themselves count. As Steven A. Culbertson, CEO of Youth Service America (which coordinates the day's events in the United States), tells us, for at least this one day in mid-April, youth around the world answer back to the catcalls that would have us and them believe they are worthless.

We don't, however, need to look to billionaires or national organizations to find the seeds of compassion growing. They are within view in every community if we care to look. Even in problem-plagued neighborhoods where gun violence and dropout rates are increasing, there are efforts afoot by youth themselves to give young people a voice, hope, and a safer future. Youth workers regularly organize events for young people and keep their recreational facilities open late so that youth who want something other than a life of gangs and violence have the choice. Once inside the recreation center, youth find mentors, diversions such as music and sports, and a sense of themselves as part of a community where they are welcomed.

Pulitzer Prize–winning reporter Sydney Schanberg, whose book *The Death and Life of Dith Pran* was the basis for the movie *The Killing Fields*, has hope for the next generation. In the fall of 2001, after a distinguished forty-year career as a journalist, he offered the convocation speech at the State University of New York at New Paltz. He spoke of his own past, growing up during the Second World War, and of the sacrifices people made during that time. He said, passionately, "You felt like you were a part of something bigger than yourself, something you didn't quite understand but nonetheless made you feel relevant, useful, not just looking out for yourself." He challenged his audience to learn from that time:

> I'm willing to bet that a whole bunch of you feel the same way. You want to be valuable—not just successful for yourself and your families, but valuable and feeling good about yourselves. What you face now is a great opportunity. . . . You can become not just another version of the several "me" generations, but instead a new "we" generation. The beginnings of this possibility have already been witnessed in the World Trade Center tragedy and its aftermath. People have taken risks for others without hesitation. People have come together more than they had in a long time. People have volunteered for community service. The question is: Can we sustain these new beginnings, keep them going? Or will we soon slip back into lazy ways, into self-indulgence and instant gratification? . . . And now you,

this generation of graduates, have had the baton passed to you. You've been given the chance to pick us up and lead us through this mess we're in, this hate, this plague. I honestly envy you. I also honour you. Imagine the chance of being named the "We" generation.[6]

If we look for the We Generation, we will find it. If we want to transform rude children into caring contributors, we can. Like Christina, the kids have told me they are waiting for an invitation from us adults to be a part of our families and communities. We need to ask ourselves, What are we doing to help or hinder a We Generation define itself?

Our Children Need to Know They Count

Why, with so much potential to know each other and communicate, and amid an explosion of information and shared wisdom, are some children still acting so irresponsibly? The answer might make us uneasy. Through my work, I get to meet hundreds of families and their children. They are teaching me that our children want to find in their communities a place where they are heard and feel they belong. Denied those experiences, dangerous, delinquent, deviant, and disordered behaviors make a satisfying substitute. There are always gangs, sex, drugs, crime, and street life to turn to as places where one can feel connected.

In our families, or beyond our front porches, our children want to be wrapped in a silky cocoon of purpose and place.

They want to know they count.

So very much of what they want can only be found when the adults who care for them are a part of their lives. Despite the buzz of electronic gadgetry, the expanding horizons of globalization, or the addiction of endless choice in fashion and entertainment, our children need their attachments with adults to create a secure sense of who they are. If we don't want our children wandering aimless and lonely on the Internet, falling prey to predators, annihilating themselves on drugs, or becoming bullies and bystanders who squash others' self-respect to make themselves feel whole, then we are going to have to reconnect with our kids. Compassion is ours to teach.

The kids tell me that their salvation has always been, and still is, their connections with their parents and other important caregivers. They want real connections: the breezy love of a passing hug, or the eye contact made with a parent sitting in the audience during a sixth-grade concert. They value our signature on a test they bring home to get signed; they may groan, but they want to hear our stories over dinner, and they want us to hear theirs; and of course, they want to spend time with us when tears need to be shed and anger forgiven.

The child who has all of that is the one most ready to deal with cyber-bullies, Internet porn, the onslaught of front-page war stories, or the indignities of always feeling compared with the next superstar on *American Idol*. The child who knows our compassion also understands she is part of a family and community that values her. From such roots, responsible children grow.

Unfortunately, many families, like Christina's, whether rich, poor, white, black, Native American, or Asian, are struggling to make these intimate connections with their children. Many of the barriers we encounter are our own doing: Monster homes, overly regulated schools with no-touch policies, suburban wastelands of impersonal spaces, a drive-through culture, mass media, too much screen time, fast food, and the disintegrating boundaries around our nuclear families are all chiseling away at family connections.

What can't we blame?

I'm not here to blame. Instead, I'd like to share the ways families have found to connect with their children, and to extend invitations to young people to act responsibly and show concern for the well-being of others. These families' answers to these challenges are often inelegant and frequently conceived under pressure. They're never perfect. But they work. They work because, in every case, as these families have taught me, our children want to experience another's compassion toward them. And it is from that experience of unconditional caring that young people learn responsibility for themselves and others.

It's Up to All of Us

The question we need to ask ourselves as parents is whether we are raising our children to be a We Generation or another bunch of Me-thinkers like ourselves.

The good news is that children want to act differently from their parents and to be in relationships with them. So we need to listen to young people. We need to know that parents still make a difference as to whether children choose the path of selfishness or choose to contribute. Across our communities, there are too many youth being raised without the benefit of someone who can show them what it means to think We. When we abdicate our role as our children's guides, or model for them self-centeredness, the results are disastrous, as in these three scenarios:

1. A sixth-grade teacher asks her pupils, "Please take your seat." One student rolls her eyes at her teacher and keeps

talking. When the teacher asks again, the youngster tells her, "Stop picking on me. I don't have to listen to you." Then the girl goes out to the hall and gets a drink of water before returning to class and taking her seat. Exasperated, the teacher calls the girl's parents that evening. "Yes," her father says. "My daughter told me all about what happened. I don't approve of you raising your voice to my child. If it happens again, we'll bring this up with your principal." The teacher is so flabbergasted she says nothing. Hanging up, she wonders what trouble is in store for her.

2. The movie is rated fourteen and older, but the unaccompanied minors aren't acting their age. During the show, they talk and answer cell phones. They get up from their seats every few minutes, running in pairs up to the lobby or switching seats with other kids at the back of the theater. When the attendant tells them to be quiet, they stop talking for a few minutes, but then are right back at it. When the man next to me yells, "Shut up!" they giggle even louder. But we can do nothing more without the children's parents to complain to.

3. The dental hygienist in the next room is politely making small talk with her fifteen-year-old patient. "Where do you go to school, honey?" she asks. "Do you take the bus to get here?" "What classes at school are you missing today?" The young woman barks out short answers. "Yes." "No." After the third question, the patient sighs dismissively. "What are you doing, writing a book?" she says sharply. The hygienist flushes red and goes about her work quietly.

Helping our children learn to feel compassion for others and to act responsibly is an old-fashioned idea that needs revisiting. As parents, we needn't feel like failures or imagine our children to be incorrigible and lost like the children I just described. There is in fact much to celebrate about youth today. I can actually see lots of advantages to today's emphasis on parenting our children to think for themselves, to challenge unjust rules, to take chances, and to be seen and heard in their communities.

I just don't want them to become belligerent and rude. As satirist Evelyn Waugh wrote a half century ago, "What is youth except a man or a woman before it is ready and fit to be seen?" It's up to us to get our children ready.

I want them to know how to show genuine kindness toward others. I don't want them to fake being nice. Even psychopaths can be nice. Being nice is nothing more than hiding your true feelings behind altruism. It is being good to others for your own sake.

I want my children to demonstrate enlightened self-interest. The girl in the hygienist's chair is not being kind to a woman who is trying to do her work competently. The patient is not even being very nice to her. She's also not making the world a happier, safer, more caring place for herself or any other child who next sits in that chair.

If we don't want children to act like these little monsters, we are going to have to accept some responsibility as their parents for raising them to act otherwise. Our children's sense of entitlement, their belligerence and lack of civility, is something parents can influence. It is never too late to help our children understand what we expect of them.

Today's Child

Fortunately, if we look, we will see the We Generation all around us. There are telltale signs they are here. Members of a We Generation:

- *Connect with their "herd"*: They value their relationships as places to share something unique about themselves.
- *Think local, act local:* Their flesh-and-blood relationships matter to them. They feel committed to shaping those relationships in ways that meet their needs for connections.
- *Think global, act global:* Their connections are also electronic. They revel in their connectivity and the global scope of their awareness. They understand trends, but also feel like contributors to those trends through their own postings onto the Web.
- *Consume with conscience:* They are aware of their complicity in the state of the world and are interested in having a say over how and what they consume. Today's young people think about "fair trade" and child labor, eating locally, and the ethics of environmental degradation.
- *Assert their individuality, and respect others for doing the same:* Identities are fluid. Young people are willing to experiment with a large number of possibilities that reach far beyond what's available at home.
- *Think about friends more than possessions:* Though owning things is still important, youth's possessions are only really valued if there is an audience to share them with. A new purse, a new suntan, a new pet, or vacation photos are all made more important when shared. In the contest between mass consumption and friendships, friendships trump endlessly working to buy meaningless things.
- *Value responsibility:* Members of this generation want and need to feel a part of their families and communities. They want roots, wings, and an audience to appreciate

them. They want spaces opened for them where they can belong and give back.

Christina: Take Two

Christina, the young woman we met earlier in this introduction, wants to be a part of a We Generation. It's up to her parents, though, to help her feel connected. But that will only happen if they accept the role they must play. That includes understanding that for all of Christina's advantages, she isn't finding what she needs.

From the outside, her life looks great. She's got a Barbie Doll pretty face, clothes in her closet, cute curtains on her windows, and at least one parent at home asleep most nights. It would all work if it weren't so devoid of attachments. She lives with her parents, but she hasn't really been a part of their lives for months. In the morning, she wakes up very late. Her mother has gone to play tennis, and her father is gardening. The kitchen is empty. She pours herself a glass of juice and gets a bowl of cereal. Her parents are taking a stand against processed sugars these days, so there's no Cocoa Puffs, her favorite. Just organic "crap" that tastes like sawdust. She's complained, but they've insisted she should appreciate what she's given. She eats a few mouthfuls, then dumps the soggy mess into the sink.

She sneaks a few dollars from her parents' change dish. Grabs the hat she likes from the living room couch, where she left it the night before. On the way out of the house, she passes her father, who is in the front garden. He waves at her, his work glove clumped with soil. Christina stops. Waits for the third degree.

Paul, her father, stands up amid the rhododendrons he was replanting. "They need more light," he says awkwardly to his daughter.

She rolls her eyes. Barks, "Whatever."

Paul says nothing for a moment; he's shy talking with his daughter. He wants to know where she is going, when she'll be back. Christina senses his confusion. "I'll be back by dinner," she says. It's a lie, and they both know it.

Paul wants to say something else to his daughter. He'd love it if she'd come over and admire the garden. He'd like her to bring her friends home, too. He wants her to know she matters. But it feels too late now. He is away too much these days to really connect. He doesn't even know who her friends are, or what they like doing. He couldn't name one of them if he tried. A shame, he thinks. Their house is so beautiful, now, what with the new gardens and all. It gets used so seldom by anyone but him and his wife. "Why isn't my daughter happy?" he wonders every evening that he returns home and doesn't find her there.

Seeing her walk away, he suddenly feels just as empty as the boxy Cape Cod behind him. He puts down his shovel. If he stops to reconsider, he knows he'll do nothing and just keep gardening, hiding from his feelings. So he quickly blurts out to Christina, "I bet you haven't had much breakfast. I've noticed you've barely been eating anything. What do you say we go out for breakfast? I wouldn't mind a plate of Benny's greasy eggs. Maybe some bacon? You can have the French toast with syrup if you like."

Christina doesn't move. She would actually like to go for breakfast. She would like to tell her dad about what happened last night. She'd like to eat fattening food and remember that there was a time when she and her parents used to know each other better.

But her friends are waiting.

She starts to shake her head and say something smart, like "Thanks, but no thanks," but her dad looks down at his feet, says "Christina . . . " He doesn't often use her name. Somehow their conversation has become a stream of commands, directions, details, but never names. She likes the way he says her name.

"Christina," he says again, "I miss you." The words seem so trivial to him. They are mumbled to the flowers. His words land ill planted, unseasonable.

Christina flushes.

She will say later that breakfast never tasted so good. She'll thank her father for never once telling her what to do, for never once lecturing her. She appreciated that he talked with her like a real person. He told her about his last trip to New York and the black limo he saw with all the security people around it and how it looked just like those you see in the movies. And when she opened a second plastic tub of syrup for her French toast, he raised no complaint. He just asked the waitress to bring some more.

When they got home and had parked the Lexus in the driveway, Paul turned shy again. He told her, "I had better get back to the garden, while the weather's good." He didn't really know what else to say.

Christina got out of the car, said a quiet "Thank you for breakfast," and then started down the driveway. Before she reached the sidewalk, she turned to look back at her dad.

"I'll be back by dinner," she said. This time both she and Paul knew it might be true.

chapter **one**

Parents Matter

We all want our children to grow up and make their mark. We want them to make a contribution to society for which they will be remembered. Call it pride or hubris, but we are compelled as parents to want our children to leave the world a little bit better place for their efforts. I think we have always wanted our children to think We instead of Me.

Wouldn't it be wonderful, we dream, if it were our offspring who fixed global warming? Who ended wars? Who discovered a cure for AIDS?

Whether our kids become caring, competent contributors to their communities, both locally and globally, will depend a great deal on what we as parents provide them. Christina is at a turning point. Either she will drift further into recklessness and disorder, or she will find someone to show her compassion. She will learn responsibility, or she will learn to think only about herself. Our children's futures depend on what adults teach them.

And, reassuringly, it's the small things we do that count the most, for example, the way we insist our children take responsibility for helping to clean the house or the way we expect them to care for us when we're ill or just plain tired. The decisions we make about the car we drive and the house we own teach our children about what's really important and what's not. Where we travel for our annual vacation and whom we invite into our homes show our children what it means to be tolerant of others and respectful of differences. If we really want to raise a generation of kids who think beyond themselves, the solution is near at hand. It rests with us and how we spend our time with our children. What we show them. What they hear us say. How we model for them a life lived with meaning.

The compassion we show them and others, and the responsibility we expect them to show toward others and themselves, become templates for how they will live their lives. Thinking about how this is done and the meaning of compassion, I find it impossible not to think of the exiled fourteenth Dalai Lama of Tibet. Forced to flee his kingdom and the red palace that sits majestically on a hill in the center of old Lhasa when the Chinese invaded Tibet in 1950, the boy leader never became bitter over the destruction of more than three thousand monasteries. Today, with the planned Dalai Lama Center for Peace and Education, a Vancouver center dedicated to promoting kindness, compassion, and interconnectedness through research, education, and dialogue, the Dalai Lama continues to offer some loving solutions to world-sized problems. It is his goal to encourage caring, peace, and tolerance and to embrace all humanity as brothers and sisters, even the Chinese people whom he believes, individually, meant him no harm. "For that," he says, "compassion is needed."[1]

The next generation suffers no flaws that we adults can't help fix. There are abundant guides to help us. Just as the Dalai Lama and other great leaders from history such as Mahatma Gandhi and Martin Luther King Jr. teach us, there is no problem in this world too great for the next generation to solve.

Imagine how the scenarios with those three children I mentioned in the introduction might play out if their parents (and the other adults involved) showed their love by holding them accountable:

1. When the sixth-grade teacher calls a student's home to talk about her rudeness, the girl's father asks for the three of them to meet. After that meeting, knowing his daughter walked out on the teacher, he tells his daughter, "That is not the way to handle conflict. I don't know which of you is telling the truth here, but how you solved the problem made you look rude and immature. If you have something constructive to say about your teacher, tell me, and I'll bring it up with her. But acting rudely toward her is not the solution."

2. The movie attendant remains at the back of the theater after he tells the teens to quiet down. When they start acting up again, he gets a second attendant to help him remove them from the theater. The youth are barred from the theater for four months. Their parents are called as well and told what happened. The parents are understandably embarrassed, but let their children suffer the natural consequences of their actions.

3. After being so rudely spoken to by a fifteen-year-old, the hygienist stops what she is doing and tells the girl, "Honey, I was just trying to make you feel comfortable here. That's my job. But it's also something I'm proud of doing.

You don't need to speak to me like that. If you're having a bad day, that's okay. We don't have to talk. But I just wanted to let you know I was trying to make you feel comfortable. You understand?" The girl nods and looks anywhere but into the kindly eyes of the woman in front of her. Later, as the hygienist explains the bill to the girl's mother, she mentions what happened during the cleaning. During the drive home, the girl's mother asks her daughter, "Anything you want to tell me?" Her daughter is too embarrassed to speak.

A generation or two ago, each of these situations would probably have been handled differently. The sixth-grade teacher and the father would have told the girl to blindly obey her teacher. Those kids in the theater would have been kicked out forever. The fifteen-year-old would have been told she was being rude by both the hygienist and her mother, without any consideration for the kind of day the girl might have been having. And the boy whom I mentioned in the preface and who swore at his principal when the man gave him a friendly greeting on the road might have had his mouth washed out with soap.

In my work, I meet lots of kids who are kept in line through threats and punishments. It doesn't work; even when it appears to work for a while, the results are children who obey but can't think for themselves. They grow up selfish and self-centered. "How can I avoid punishment?" they think. "When will I be big enough to get my own way?"

I'm certainly not going to advocate for punishment that makes things worse. But I'd welcome a little more community support for parents and a willingness among parents to let our children understand the consequences of their actions.

Spirited Parenting

As parents, we can appreciate what we do well when we take the time to notice our success. A growing trend in organizational research is called appreciative inquiry (AI). AI encourages us to look at what we are doing right instead of at our failings. If we want to find solutions to problems, we need to know our strengths.

Somehow, though, we forget to notice exactly what we're doing right as parents. We notice the one Thanksgiving dinner when our moody twelve-year-old sulks, forgetting the year before, when we encouraged him (successfully) to help in the kitchen. We get upset with our "irresponsible" daughter whose bicycle was left out overnight and stolen, forgetting that the week before, we drove her and that same bicycle to a local park for a cyclethon to raise money for our children's hospital.

Judy Johnson, a group facilitator who has worked with the United Nations and other international organizations, uses AI in workshops with parents. As she explains, "Parenting is a huge adventure, full of peak experiences. Many of us did not know what we had signed up for until we experienced it directly. A spirited parent is one who embraces the journey, who trusts his own judgment, takes risks, and learns together with his children."

Working together with Judy and her colleagues Kim Wilson and Shannon Aikenhead-Bain, I've discovered that parents both want and need to be reminded of their successes. Try the following for yourself:

1. Remember an inspired parenting moment, a situation where you felt you were tested but rose to the challenge, when you felt invigorated. Now describe the situation.

- What was happening?
- What were you thinking and feeling?
- What was your child doing?
- What makes this situation memorable for you?

2. We don't succeed in our roles as parents alone. Raising a We Generation is too big a task for any one person. Thinking back to your successful, spirited moment as a parent, ask yourself:

- What helped you respond in an inspired manner?
- What conditions supported or created this parenting moment (a specific mental attitude, a certain behavior, or some external support)?
- What will you need to do to have a similar moment happen again?

The Boomer's Individualism

Baby boomers (they're us or our parents) grew up with an abundance of job opportunities and an antiauthoritarian streak that was forged in the fires of political resistance, cultural imperialism, and racial struggles. People began to think about their personal liberties and the supremacy of reason over tradition and prejudice. Somewhere along the line, amid the bounty of the postwar era, my generation forgot about sacrifice or commitment to a cause. We forgot about the herd.

I laugh now to recall meeting Joni Mitchell at a bar in the mountains of Alberta in the early 1980s. I asked her whose music she liked, and she answered, "My own." It was the perfect answer for a generation raised to think about themselves, and so very different from a generation today who can be inspired by a universe of millions of small-name bands who can post their tunes on the Internet.

Ironically, it has been our collectivist ways (exemplified by the emergence of the welfare state and social programs) that have made it possible to be a little more individualistic. Children today may appear like spoiled brats, when in fact they are young people assuming responsibility for their lives. For example, we may see many of them remaining in our basements long after the age we ourselves moved out. They can do that because there is less rush today for young people to finish their education and settle for careers for which they lack passion. Far from being mindless drifters, the majority of twentysomethings I meet tell me they are exploring opportunities or making their way into careers slowly, trying to avoid the financial traps their parents fell into.[2] Even during tough economic times, a job market that pushes them into menial work and doesn't ask them to use their skills makes it attractive to "slack off" for a time. Are they being selfish? Not necessarily.

It's all a bit of a paradox. After all, many of the needs of our children are met by the collective. They can afford to be a little standoffish and indulge their uniqueness because when it comes right down to it, they are already woven into the fabric of their communities. There is a social contract of care and compassion that was put in place after the Second World War, even if the contract is one we forever threaten to tear asunder.

To Act or Not to Act?

The biggest change our children are experiencing is the information revolution, which is making community participation both possible and expected. Take, for example, the problem of global warming. Our kids have taken note of the need to go green. They have noticed the hypocrisy of their elders who recycle milk cartons but drive Buick Navigators. They understand that change has to happen, and they are assuming responsibility for that change. Slowly. They are making choices, and they are vocal (and occasionally arrogant and rude) about the responsibility they feel to fix the mistakes of generations past.

Skeptical? Look around your community, and you are likely to find children who are part of Green Teams at school. Raising money for the World Wildlife Fund. Petitioning for bike lanes on city streets. Arguing with their parents about spraying pesticides and herbicides on their lawns. Worrying about whales. Wondering if they'll ever see an iceberg. Concerned with the environmental impact of industrial farming and overgrazing. They understand concepts that, a generation ago, were on the fringes at best: Mathis Wackernagel and William Rees's ecological footprint; Norwegian ecophilosopher Arne Næss's deep ecology; Frances Moore Lappé's food sustainability. Even young children watching Animal Planet know that cars pollute and that the rain forest is shrinking (and with it our earth's biodiversity). This is a generation weaned on Discovery television, and the antics of the late Australian crocodile "hunter" and passionate conservationist Steve Irwin (and his daughter, Bindi). This generation's consciousness is arguably far greater than any generation's before it.

Of course, changes in attitudes don't necessarily mean changes in behavior. That's where parents come in. Our kids need us to help enable them to make those changes. It's still parents who give their children the green light to go green.

Saying Yes to the Kids

The child who is admonished for thinking for himself will never move from bystander to savior. Raising a We Generation means avoiding the imposition of too many rules. It means saying yes more than no.

There is good science to justify parenting more by example and encouragement than by strictly enforced rule books. We know that children are particularly susceptible to sticking to the rules when it comes to helping others. In 1969, Ervin Staub showed that seventh-graders who were told not to enter the room next to theirs would hesitate to go and help someone whom they could hear had just had an accident.[3] In other words, rules can inhibit our actions. The same is true in a quite different scenario; a few notorious experiments about obedience to authority in the 1950s by Stanley Milgram showed that people will inflict pain on others if told to do so.[4]

We know that children who are encouraged rather than forced to help tend to help more, even when not being supervised by their caregivers. It really is a case of "teach your children well," and they will do unto others as they would have others do unto them. Saying yes to our children obligates us as parents to show them how to behave, and it reinforces the prosocial behaviors they will need in a world gone global.

Compassion cannot be taught through punishment. We cannot tell our children what to do all the time and then expect them to be proactive when their help is needed. The child punished for not helping comes to associate helping with anger. We know that angry, unhappy people help less often than happy people. If we want our children to show responsible behavior toward others, then we need to reward them for the help they give and we need to encourage them to offer what help they can. If they have hurt someone, or failed to offer help when it was needed, it is better to remind them of their obligations and insist they fulfill those obligations than to berate them for their failings.

Say your child refuses to set the dinner table when it's her turn. If you want to avoid raising a spoiled child, then it is best to hold your daughter accountable for her decision. "Fine," you say. "Since I cooked, and you haven't contributed, then maybe you can cook for yourself tonight." This isn't simple tit for tat. It's about respecting your child's right to self-determination. With responsibility come consequences. In this case, it may mean a peanut butter and jam sandwich supper when everyone else is eating chicken stir fry. Try that for a few evenings, especially if the next night you prepare the youngster's favorite dinner (baked ham with mashed potatoes and steamed carrots glazed in honey), and see if table setting doesn't quickly seem a reasonable contribution to her family.

There is reciprocity to helping others. Like compassion, it pays forward. Those who are helped and given opportunities and encouragement to help others will amplify the effect by doing good deeds later on. It is as if the compassion we show our children is a seed that grows and blossoms. Not unlike the many offshoots that branch off our family trees, many acts of kindness may be inspired by that first thoughtful act. At least, it can happen when the conditions are right for growth.

If you allow a child to take and take and you provide no opportunities or expectations for him to give back to his family or community, you will create a selfish egoist. Narcissism can turn into disorder. The narcissistic child thinks only Me, never We.

It is still all about our parenting. If we volunteer, our children volunteer. If we give blood, our children are more likely to give blood. They learn from us what compassion means in practice.

Ages and Stages

The lesson of how to put compassion into practice follows distinct stages. In other words, what motivates us to help changes with age:

- The toddler thinks, "Because Mom/Dad said . . . " No matter how progressive we are in our thinking, toddlers need direction. They need to be told what to do if they are to act responsibly. "Your sister is crying. Give her a kiss." "Pick your toys up so I don't trip over them." "Share." Part of our role as parents is to socialize our children, to tame their natural impulse to harm others or to act selfishly. Often, the toddler needs to be reminded of the consequences of his behavior. He needs to be shown the damage he has caused (another child's tears) or to be shown how he can make up for his mistakes (by sharing his own toys when he's broken another child's). Natural consequences that benefit others and undo one's mistakes help to teach a child empathy. Threats of punishment, however, are unlikely to help raise a compassionate child. They produce only a child who understands that the bigger you are, the bossier you can be. The child who is ordered to be nice and threatened with a spanking if he does otherwise isn't learning compassion. He learns to do things for others as a form of self-preservation.
- The five- to seven-year-old thinks, "I want to help." Ask an elementary-school child for help, and she is likely to feel pleased with being asked. There is something about a big person relying on a little person that makes the little person feel good about

herself. There is no need to compel children to help. They want to help if they think their helping will get them recognition.

- The eight- to ten-year-old thinks, "I'll help you if you'll help me." Children figure out soon enough that helping others is a good way to curry favors. There is a tangible reward for the child who helps. While what we see is apparent reciprocity, the child's motivation to help is driven by a selfish understanding of the world: Being nice to others gets you further than being selfish. Developmentally, that's okay for now. Eventually, the principle of doing good deeds will be internalized and the child will act compassionately toward others for no greater payoff than personal satisfaction.

- The eleven- to twelve-year-old thinks, "Because that's the rule." Ah, the blessed tweens. By this point, a well-socialized child who has experienced the give-and-take of loving relationships understands the rules of social engagement. I scratch your back, you scratch mine, and everyone feels good. The tween understands that good behavior brings social approval. For a time, at least, the world is a predictable place where good deeds get noticed.

- The thirteen- to fifteen-year-old thinks, "Hey, look at me!" The young adolescent seeks social approval for playing the good child. There needn't be any tangible gain. A simple nod and the assurance that the child is noticed and matters is all that he wants in order to do something good for someone else.

- The sixteen- to nineteen-year-old thinks, "Let's all just get along." The older youth expects that her actions will foster good deeds by others. She has a naive expectation that the world is a good place and people who have been treated kindly will happily be kind to one another. The world is politically simple, and social problems solvable. The youth thinks, "Why can't we just get along?"

- The young adult thinks, "I help because I like to help." By young adulthood, the youth raised with compassion intuitively understands the benefits to helping others. The young adult values altruism because he wants to feel the self-esteem and personal satisfaction that come with knowing he has helped. Is it any wonder we are so passionate in our love of our partners at this age? So ready to risk our lives for our countries? We are high on the feeling of giving. Ready and now able to help others, at this stage we seek only the warm embrace of spiritual connection when we forgo our personal welfare for the welfare of others. The gains we expect are entirely internal, a feeling more than a tangible reward.

The ages and stages I have outlined are, of course, fluid. Children move through these stages at their own pace. While many children advance in a pattern similar to what I've just described, many others move faster or slower.

As Jean Piaget, the renowned human developmental theorist, showed many years ago, children develop in small bursts their ability to appreciate the feelings of others.[5] Children below the age of five can rarely understand another's perspective. Instead, they reason that others experience the world in just the same way they do: "If I like chocolate, then everyone must like chocolate. If I'm sad, everyone must be sad—or I'll at least try to make them sad!"

Not all of us grow in our capacity to appreciate the feelings or needs of others. Our moral development may become arrested at any point. There are many adults who still seek tangible rewards for helping. Many others in our jails and institutions know only that they must be nice to others or else suffer consequences. Similarly, there are elementary-school children who are kind beyond measure. Something inside compels them to give of themselves with no expectation of return. Perhaps their wisdom comes from having lived past lives, as a Buddhist might say, or they are blessed by an angel, as Christians might speculate. Or maybe they have the right temperament and have been well parented (the dry, theoretical retort of the existential agnostic). Regardless, such children grow at an exponential rate in their capacity to give.

In fact, that capacity to act kindly toward others replaces the aggression that children have naturally. Richard Tremblay, a developmental psychologist, has shown that we are never so violent as when we are two-year-olds biting and scratching.[6] Tremblay has shown that children don't become violent. They are born aggressive and then gradually socialized out of bad behavior and into good. There is no innocent, peaceful state of childhood bliss, only small, cherub-cheeked people whose aggressive actions have fewer consequences for themselves and others.

All Together Now

We display compassion in our homes—through touch, connections, and other simple expressions of love. That demonstration extends to our schools, where we hope our children are shown respect and taught more than their ABCs; we hope they will be taught about others and our responsibilities toward one another.

To teach compassion is to instill in our children a sense of cohesion, a feeling of being their brothers' and sisters' keepers, as responsible for the welfare of others as they are for their own. It also means providing children with opportunities to experience these connections. That means a chance to work or volunteer, to give something back. To fulfill a meaningful role as part of something bigger. To find an identity as someone's benefactor. To know, tangibly, "Here is where I belong." The model of compassion extends even further to their nations, where the unglamorous world of social policy is enacted in ways that say we give a damn about our kids. We don't leave them messes we ourselves couldn't clean up. We don't leave them burdensome debts. We don't underfund their education, their child-care, their safety, their medical care. The model stretches to encompass what children might experience when they cross borders and cultures. Compassion is learned through their interaction with others who are different from them. It is found in small moments of sharing and long periods of living side by side.

But as much as we want our schools to teach these things, learning about compassion starts at home. Without those first experiences, our children are useless navigating school, community, nation, globe. We need to be thinking big these days. Our kids' world is too small for parents to focus exclusively on what's happening in our own backyard, on our street, or just around the corner.

The foundation stones for the We Generation are found in many houses across many cultures. The Old Testament stresses benevolence, according to the Talmudic commentaries written centuries ago by Jewish scholars. Psalm 112 tells us: "They have distributed freely, they have given to the poor; their righteousness endures forever." In the Qur'an, too, there is great emphasis placed on the need for Muslims to give to the poor and ensure the well-being of others. Zakah is one of the five pillars of Islam and requires each member of the faith to give a prescribed percentage of the person's wealth to those less fortunate in order to alleviate their suffering until such time that they can themselves be independent. Thus, Muslims are told: "Be kind to parents, and the near kinsman, and to orphans, and to the needy, and to the neighbor who is of kin, and to the neighbor who is a stranger, and to the companion at your side, and to the traveller."

Christian faith emphasizes the same idea, with the tithe, a payment of money and wealth to the church so that it might look after those less fortunate. Proverbs 22 tells us: "Rob not the poor, because he is poor; neither oppress the afflicted in the gate: For the Lord will plead their cause, and spoil the soul of those that spoiled them." Chinese philosophies share this same thread of benevolence. Confucius tells us in the *Analects* that youth "should overflow in love to all, and cultivate the friendship of the good" and that the virtuous man "who acts with a constant view to his own advantage will be much murmured against." Similarly, the Buddha told his followers that even small acts of generosity were a path to enlightenment. In the Dhammapada 224, the author writes that the Buddha entreated devotees to "give even from a scanty store to him who asks."

And so on and so on. Generation after generation, we share with our children such wisdom.

While these ideas have influenced how human beings have related one to another for millennia, the harbingers of the We Generation's collective sense of well-being came during the Second World War. This was a time when responsibility meant action and sacrifice. A just war justified courage. Nations came together to fight against tyranny. There was no false intelligence, or cynicism; there really was a need for action and contribution. Perhaps because this war was considered necessary (even the defeated now consider the battles necessary, except maybe for the Allied carpet bombing and nuclear devastation), the veterans find honor in their sacrifice.

The importance of our connections with others never faded, though a sense of our obligation to their well-being has sometimes been obscured by a cultish belief in selfishness. Still, there is much good to reminisce about.

During the 1960s, a generation of young people said *enough* to war and racial segregation. In the 1980s, it was the arms race and the doctrine of mutual assured destruction that compelled youth to take to the streets. I remember joining a million others, many of them students, on the streets of New York City in 1982 to protest nuclear proliferation. We choked the city closed, coursed through the streets, overflowed onto sidewalks, squeezed between one glass building and another, chanting impassioned slogans. Like many of my generation and those before me, we felt we had to do something.

"What do we want?" we shouted.

"Disarmament!"

"When do we want it?"

"*Now!*"

We still have nuclear bombs. The Cold War has been replaced by a different kind of ethnic conflict. We still export violence from the West, creating the small arms that make it possible for child soldiers to be drafted by paramilitaries and terrorists. While those things haven't changed, we are today a much smaller and more interconnected world. Our children understand this perhaps better than we ever did.

Former president Bill Clinton says we have been living in a period of interdependence.[7] Our actions influence others on a global scale. Our interdependence, Clinton says, can be positive or negative. If we forgive the debts of African nations, we allow them more money for education and health care. That it was our oppressive International Monetary Fund that in many cases bankrupted those nations and lowered their standard of living in the first place is conveniently overlooked. That Tanzania, for example, was better off before it took massive development loans is something the bureaucrats don't like to talk about. But there is no denying that the better our neighbors do, the safer we all are. Poverty breeds violence. I prefer to follow my children's lead. They seem to look beyond color and culture. They may not have the solutions to world peace and good government—yet—but they understand that the world is much smaller and more interdependent than I, for one, ever imagined it to be. As Clinton reminds us, "our interests are always converging."

Even a notion like interdependence, however, isn't going to capture all of what our children are experiencing. Interdependence conjures images of two separate and distinct bodies choosing to work together.

We are no longer so distinct. We cannot choose to remain separate. Clinton says that when we share a sense of belonging and think about our neighbors and not just our own tribe, we move from interdependence to an integrated community. While the rules of order in that new integrated world may be different from those of our post–Second World War utopias, parents are still vital to preparing their children to participate in those integrated communities. How our children navigate their way through the myriad of relationships they find there will largely reflect the compassion they learn from us. If they are to take responsibility in the global exchange, they are going to have to experience accountability for their actions at home and at school.

Giving a damn about others, our country, even our planet, is seldom possible without a foundation of love from a parent. All our children's electronic interdependence becomes nothing but noise without a parent's compassionate guidance. Facts and ideas coursing through the electronic pipe are easily ignored by children who know nothing of compassion for others or their own role in making their world a better place.

From Compassion to Action

If we've done our job well, our children are more likely to show compassion toward their parents and others. Our sons and daughters are likely to behave in ways we admire at school and at the mall. If we continue to be there for them as they grow, we can help show them how to act responsibly in their neighborhoods. We can convey to them the meaning of citizenship. We can teach them about people different from themselves. We can offer them opportunities to learn compassion and to demonstrate that compassion for others by acting responsibly.

At least that's what I hear from even the most troubled of youth—the most depressed, the most disenfranchised, marginalized, upset, and unhappy young people. Their eyes well with tears when I'm working with them in jails and mental-health clinics. Their voices break as they tell me how much they long for genuine flesh-and-blood, eye-to-eye connections. Over and over again, rich or poor, suburban or rural, boys and girls share with me their stories of longing for attention from a concerned parent.

It's not what we expect to hear.

We have been hearing instead much about how our children have the potential to be the most electronically connected generation ever. But if they are to take advantage of what technology has to offer, they are going to have to connect first with those who love them. Preventing our children from getting themselves into trouble still largely depends on how we parent them. We still very much matter.

Compassionate Kids

Though it's easy to see evidence of a We Generation when we meet someone of the stature of Craig Kielburger, the young man who founded the Free the Children organization, the invisible young people whom I encounter struggling to live their lives well impress me just as much.

Ryan is one such boy. He is twelve years old, but carries more responsibility than most of his peers. He's a reluctant member of the We Generation, but one just the same.

Living a distance from his school, Ryan has to take two buses to get there each morning. He's responsible for taking care of himself and his younger brother. His father, Jake, works on the oil rigs in the North Atlantic. Lately, Jake's been away three out of every four weeks. Ryan's mother, Elke, is an office manager in the industrial park. The bus she takes to her workplace goes in a direction opposite to where her children are headed.

I met Ryan when he was suspended for three days because of a comment he'd made about his seventh-grade teacher. When a friend of his was called back into the classroom after being dismissed, Ryan had teased, "She probably wants to feel you up." That and a few other incidents earned him time out at home.

His parents were understandably distraught, especially when it became clear that Ryan wasn't doing very well in most of his classes. The school was warning that he might not pass his grade or might be streamed into a classroom for children with behavioral problems.

Meeting Ryan, it would be easy to think, "This kid needs some serious consequences, lots of structure, and discipline." But none of that would have helped, because Ryan already understood the consequences to his actions. He knew he was at risk of failing, or of being labeled a problem child. He knew how upset both of his parents were with him. He had been given rules and responsibilities. What Ryan didn't have was his parents' gaze, nor anyone else's, for that matter.

Ryan was searching for a place to belong. He wanted to be a respected part of his family. His problems weren't that he was a bad kid. He wasn't trying to get himself excluded. Like many of his generation, he wanted a bigger role in family matters and more recognition beyond his front door for his contribution.

"Can you tell me what happened? About the episode with your teacher?" I asked Ryan when he and his mother met with me in my office. Wearing a T-shirt and jeans that were slipping off his hips, Ryan was your average-looking boy with uncombed, short, brown hair. Elke was dressed crisply. Beneath her eyes were dark lines that even her makeup couldn't hide. I could smell the lingering smoke of her last cigarette, which I imagined she must have had just before coming in to see me. She looked nervous, expectant.

"I was just joking," Ryan said.

"You weren't trying to get yourself expelled?" I asked. I never assume I understand a child's motivation for misbehavior. It's best to open space for the youngster to tell me what he thinks.

"No," was all Ryan said.

I paused, sensing his embarrassment. I asked him how he saw the suspension. Was it a good thing or bad?

"A bad thing," he said looking at his mother. Then, turning his face back to me, told me, "But not much of a problem."

"He did say that he was worried, and embarrassed," Elke said. "We've talked some about it."

The fact that they'd talked was a good sign. I asked a few more questions about the comment. I wondered aloud why he made that particular comment and not another. Why something so sexually graphic?

"I didn't even think about it before I said it," Ryan answered earnestly. "I didn't think about it like that. You know. About the sex part."

I believed him. The language of boys his age is often full of taunts and teases that suggest more curiosity than understanding. I was intrigued, though, why Ryan, a child with so much responsibility, had acted so irresponsibly. Elke explained quickly the consequences that she and Jake had imposed on their son to try to straighten him out. "He lost his computer, and his PlayStation is gone, too," she said. "And when I'm not at home, he's supposed to do some reading and practice his drums." It sounded like a fair plan. Only Ryan hadn't done any of it. By this point, Ryan was looking at the floor, the palms of his hands pressed deep into his jean pockets. Frustrated, Elke explained, "I have to work. I'm not around. I can't be. We tried to get the school to do an in-school suspension, but they said there was no way that was going to happen."

"I'd prefer an in-school suspension," Ryan said. "At least then I'd see my friends."

I nodded, and we talked for a few more minutes about Ryan's experience learning, the school climate, how his friends behaved, and what they expected of Ryan. School for Ryan had never gone very well. He wasn't a strong reader. His math skills were average. He was a normal kid growing up in a world that expected excellence. What he did do well was look after his younger brother. Besides getting him to and from school, there were lunches to help prepare and bullies to avoid. His ability to look after the younger boy was never questioned.

"With your brother, it seems you do fine. You never let him get into any trouble. Is that true?" I asked.

"I sort of have to look after him," Ryan said, not recognizing the huge role he actually played in his sibling's life.

"Both his father and I really do appreciate what he does. But that's no excuse for him to misbehave at school. He should know better," Elke said.

I sat back in my chair for a minute. It's easy to get stuck when conversations circle back on themselves like this. Ryan's a good kid who should know better, so why is he blowing it at school? Maybe, I thought to myself, Ryan wants more responsibility, not less. Maybe school hasn't been beefing up his self-esteem but is actually undermining it. It was as if this very competent young man was quite capable of looking after himself and others until he reached the door of his classroom. Then what? He was reminded of his lack of capacity. How little he measured up.

"Let me ask something," I began a few moments later. "Ryan, what would you like to be learning?"

"I like to learn," he said. "But I don't do too good at it when I'm at school. I'm okay at computer games, though. Things like that."

I had guessed right, that he wanted to both learn and feel good about himself. I wondered if this might be a good time to invite Ryan to take more responsibility for the consequences of his actions, for the adults in his life to acknowledge his need to be seen as a contributor rather than an empty vessel to be filled.

"Ryan," I said, "You seem a bit old to be told what to do. Maybe it's time for you to tell the adults what you want to do and what you need. Right now, with the suspension and all, you don't look like a boy who can control his own life. But I get the sense that is exactly what you want: more control."

Ryan accepted the invitation immediately. "I don't want to do any work that I don't have to," he said. "Like at school, I only want to do homework when it's important. I don't like doing so much homework when it doesn't really count."

It seemed like a reasonable request. Elke agreed. She would speak to the school, she said, about less homework and more one-on-one support so that Ryan could do better.

"It's okay if everyone keeps on my case," Ryan said shyly. "But I don't want to have to work harder than I want to work."

That sounded fair as well, given Ryan's negative experience at school over the years.

"Are there things that your mother and father could do that would make it more likely you would succeed at school and avoid suspension?"

"Don't know," Ryan said.

"How about taking away your computer, things like that. Does that help?"

"It helps him get to his homework," said Elke. "But then after a while, it stops working. It slips again, the attitude comes back in. There's this pattern. Ryan is very oppositional to doing what he is told to do by people in authority. He's like, 'No, I don't want to do this.'"

"I don't like people who have control over me telling me what to do, that's all," Ryan said.

"I guess it's a strange age for you. You're plenty old enough to do lots of things for yourself and your younger brother, but not old enough to make every decision for yourself. Is that confusing for you?" I asked.

"Just frustrating," Ryan answered with a level of insight I'm coming to expect from the young people I meet.

Ryan went back to school the next day. There were a few changes, though, at home. First, he was told by both his parents how much they appreciated his caring for his brother. They acknowledged that anyone old enough to do all that had a right to decide how much homework he would do each evening. He still had to do some (the most important work), but they weren't going to force him into doing hours and hours of studying when it was clear Ryan was only striving for Cs and not As. Of course, not every child needs his or her parents to lower their expectations, but then not every child is struggling to cope with school as much as Ryan was. My goal, and that of his parents, was to make sure Ryan advanced to the next grade and avoided trouble. The compromises we made were strategic.

Besides lowering expectations, there were other changes as well. Most significantly, it was decided that Ryan's mother would make sure he turned off his computer and stop playing games when she came home from work at five-thirty. That would be homework time, or Ryan could do less homework but would have to come into the kitchen and help prepare dinner. We called this "learning time." One way or the other, Ryan was being given the opportunity to act responsibly.

These were all good changes, but it was one other change that most caught my attention. Ryan insisted his mother take her responsibility to him very seriously. When I met with Ryan and Elke a few weeks later Ryan explained, "Mom has to remember to tell me to turn off my computer. That's fair, right? If she asks me to do things for her and my brother, then she has to do that for me. It shows she cares."

I smiled. "And what if she forgets?" I asked, glancing only briefly at Elke.

"We thought about that," Elke said.

"I told her that there should be a consequence for her, too," Ryan said proudly. He was obviously enjoying this new role as the mature one in the family. "It should be something that helps her. So she has to pay me her cigarette money for a day. She shouldn't smoke, anyway. My dad and me tell her she'll get lung cancer. I tell her that all the time. So she has to give me ten dollars if she forgets to tell me to turn off the computer. Fair's fair, right?" It was an imaginative solution. It was also one that spoke volumes about a young person who had been shown enough compassion to return it to those who loved him.

Tips List

Sometimes it helps to provide children with suggestions for ways to practice thinking We. A box labeled "Tips for Acts of Kindness" can be left beside the dinner table, and each family member asked to draw from the box a folded piece of paper once a week. At dinner the next week, check in to see what everyone's experience has been doing what they were asked to do. How did people react when they were graced with a random act of kindness? How did it make you and your children feel? What did the children learn, about themselves and about others? Here are a few suggestions for the box. They are just as good for parents who can model We-thinking as they are for children just learning how to give of themselves to others:

- Pay someone a compliment.
- Hold the door open for the person behind you.
- Say thank you!
- Tell a friend how much you like him or her.

- Make a card for someone who needs cheering up.
- Share a treat with a friend.
- Use some money from your allowance to buy a small gift for a friend or relative.
- If someone says something mean about a student in your class (or a colleague at work), stick up for the other person.
- Tell a funny joke that will make a friend laugh.
- Give up your place at the front of the line for someone else.
- Forfeit recess one day this week to read to a younger child at school (provided your school has such a program; if not, start one!).
- Join a club like Girl Scouts, Cub Scouts, the Red Cross, or St. John's Ambulance—any group that helps people in your community when there is a crisis.
- Take out the trash without being asked.
- Do something more than your usual chores to help out around the house.
- Reduce your greenhouse gases by taking public transit to do an errand (a younger child can go with a parent or grandparent).
- Take charge of recycling in your house, in the classroom, or at work.
- Brainstorm about things that your class could do to help others in the community.
- Pick some flowers from your yard, and give them to a neighbor.
- Become a pen pal with a child in another state, either through school or through the friends of your parents.
- If a friend becomes upset over a bad grade or a missed goal in sports, tell him or her that it's okay. Remind your friend that we all have bad days, make mistakes, aren't perfect.
- Get together with friends on the weekend and build a lemonade stand; decide to what charity you'll donate the money that you earn.
- If you're in high school, organize a car wash that will raise funds for a school trip or new school equipment.

- Plant flowers or create your own garden.
- Walk the dog.
- Designate Saturday as "clean out the garage/basement/shed day."
- Recycle the toys, books, and clothes you don't need, and give them to a local charity.
- If you have a younger sibling, entertain him or her while your parents are busy.
- Give a classmate, team member, or work colleague a high five for a job well done.
- Wait till people finish talking, and don't interrupt.
- Be a mentor: Help someone younger than you with homework, or teach him or her a new skill.
- Mow the lawn or shovel the driveway for a sick or elderly neighbor—for free.
- Make a pact with your brother or sister to not argue on Mother's Day or Father's Day.
- Give a hug to someone who is having a bad day.

chapter **two**

Connected Kids

The memory of my son's birth will always be with me. He was pushed painfully out and into the waiting, gloved hands of our family doctor, then laid ever so gently on my wife's soft stomach. Outside now, but still attached by the pulsing umbilical cord. The cord was clamped. The nurse handed me surgical scissors. In what seemed too brutal a separation, I cut. I did this for both my children. Each time, I thought how odd it felt to cleave the intimacy of that first corded connection. As parents, we spend a lifetime apologizing.

Cathy and I wasted no time reassuring our son. Amid the blood- and sweat-streaked bedclothes, both of us offered him soft coos and gentle touches. We stroked each little finger (counting them, of course), then his face, his feet, his shoulders, and his double chin. The nurse eventually pried him from us for a few minutes to do her assessment. Apgar score, weight, length. He was given back to us, smelling clean and wrapped in a thick, bone-white cotton blanket. His eyes couldn't yet focus. His arms squirmed. I wondered if the noises we made were too harsh to a newborn's ears accustomed to the *wup* of liquid immersion, where time was measured not by tides but by heartbeats that drummed from above.

If psychologists such as Daniel Stern are correct, then that first experience of being outside is really not understood by babies at all.[1] That little boy in my arms had no sense yet of himself as other. There was no story there of an independent "Me," just a sensuous, strained longing for reconnection, a desire to float again in the womb's total embrace.

Warmth and cold, hunger and pain, awaken a child to differences. Within moments of his birth, my son had needs. Others were there to meet them. He depended on these caregivers. Where once there was a symbiotic connection, now there were empty spaces that needed to be negotiated.

The separation process continued, gradually. My son grew and moved from being swaddled in our arms to toddling around furniture and climbing sofas. Soon it was play dates, then preschool and elementary school. There were neatly packed lunch boxes, and backpacks, stuffed with gingerbread cookies and sip packs, that made him look oddly like a tortoise carrying his home with him. It felt as if we packed more than just food into his knapsack. We packed our hopes and dreams, sandwiched between large slices of love for that little boy. We wanted him to know we were with him even as he rifled through the bag's contents, ignoring most of what we'd left there.

Throughout those early years, we offered him a knee to cuddle on, a hug after each school day, a kiss goodnight. We embraced him with stories about a moon and a great green room and a strange boy named Sam I Am. We showed what

compassion we could for his feelings and nurtured his connections with his extended family. We taught him how to be
a good friend, to play nice, to share, to say thank you for his
birthday presents even if they weren't exactly what he
wanted. We showed him how to change the television chan-
nel, play a DVD. And we showed him how to use the computer, first with games and then with a typing tutor to
prepare him for more difficult school projects. It wasn't long
before he was teaching us how to download music, change
the ringtones on our portable phone, make a picture we took
at his ninth birthday party into a screensaver (the one of him
wrestling with all his friends on the trampoline). Then it was
MSN chat and text messaging on my cell phone (I didn't
even know I had a text feature!). Races to find information,
with him surfing the Internet while I fingered my way
through volumes of the *World Book* that now gather dust in
our family room.

A brief decade on, and the cords our child uses to nurture
himself are no longer the flesh-and-blood type of his
mother's womb, but fiber-optic. His connections are more
frequently beamed electronically as nontactile transmissions
of minute pulses of light and computer code that are still,
nostalgically, just variations of zeros and ones. Now when
my cell phone rings, it is my son telling me he has been invited to have dinner at a friend's. "Is it okay, Dad?" he asks.
I am compelled to say yes, but I miss him before the signal
ends. I tell myself he needs his wings if his family is to be his
roots. Connections and separations are now what we negoti-
ate, his life both wired and wireless, corded and cordless.

And yet, for all the technology that allows our children
to navigate their way between home and community safely,
our children still want us to be there for them. They still

want to be connected. If we are careful to leave the chair next to us in the living room unoccupied and turn the television off when our child comes home from school, odds are he will find his way to our side. He'll tell us about his life in a way that reminds us what matters. He'll say, "My friend Shawn wouldn't eat his snack and gave it to me, but Mrs. Cowan said 'No sharing,' and I had to give it back, and Shawn and me both thought that wasn't fair but didn't say anything, because Mrs. Cowan sent Jason to the office last week for talking back to her, which also wasn't fair." If we're trying to teach compassion for others, we need do nothing more than nod sympathetically. Let our child know he is heard. Tell him, "That sounds awful." Our voice pitched to the same cooing bell tone that greeted him a moment after his birth.

One Good Connection Leads to Another

If, as I'm arguing, connections at home mean connections at school, in one's neighborhood, and even globally, then we should see a pattern: We should observe children who feel empathy for members of their family acting compassionately toward classmates, teachers, the school custodian, the crossing guard. Among children taught responsibility, we are likely to see an interest in making a difference in their communities. We would expect these kids to think about global challenges such as the environment, disease, and war. We would expect them to be good family members, good students, good citizens, and conscious of the role they play as part of the human race.

It's a lot to expect.

Or is it? Isn't this exactly the kind of child we need today? Aren't these the same kind of young adults whom our parents hoped we would grow up to be? The difference today is that our children have the tools to make connections like never before, that is, if they are taught how. It is parents who can help children make the link between the compassion and responsibility they find at home and the quality of the connections they make beyond. It is a thread we can see if we look for it.

How connected are your kids? There are lots of questions you can ask yourself if you want to know just how connected your child is. Below, I've listed a few that are adapted from questionnaires given to children to assess their capacity for citizenship and their ability to participate in their communities and make a positive contribution.

Thinking about your child, answer the following questions. There is no perfect profile, no wunderkind who will impress everyone. But in beginning to think about your child as a responsible member of not only your family but also the child's school and community, we need to first consider his or her strengths. Every child has a unique pattern to how he or she handles conflict and responsibility. Our goal as parents should be to edge our children toward more responsible, compassionate behavior.

The wording of these questions describes younger teens, probably between the ages of twelve and fourteen. But you can easily adapt the questions to think about elementary-school-age children or older teens already in high school. The topics covered will be the same, though how the child expresses compassion for the needs of others or a sense of responsibility at home, school, and beyond will vary by age and context. The older teen, for example, may have a girlfriend or boyfriend, may work, or may travel independently to summer camp. The younger child is likely to be more family centered, more apt to show compassion to an aging grandparent than to someone outside the family. If the younger child is fund-raising, the money is raised for school or a sports team and, more often than not, with lots of help from parents.

The questions to ask yourself are, "Am I teaching my child enough about compassion for others?" "Am I asking my child to take responsibility for himself or herself, and for others?"

If you want to score your child, there is a key at the back of the book to the answers. Different questions score a different number of points. In general, the higher the score, the more of a We-thinker your child is. There is no perfect child profile. The questions are intended to help you identify your child's strengths and where he or she might need more mentoring.

Section One: Life at Home

1. If your child wants something done his or her way, does your child:
   a. Insist and argue, but never compromise
   b. Insist and argue, then compromise
   c. Just give in

2. You overhear your child making a joke about someone that insults that person's race or religion. What does your child do when he or she notices you listening?
   a. Repeats the joke so you can hear it
   b. Gets embarrassed and apologizes
   c. Gets angry and tells you that you shouldn't be listening
   d. Ignores you

3. Your child overhears you and your spouse talking about a relative of yours and his drinking problem. When your child next meets that relative, does your child:
   a. Avoid contact with him
   b. Look really uncomfortable but act politely
   c. Ask him why he drinks so much

4. When something good happens for someone else in the family, does your child:
   a. Ignore the accomplishment
   b. Help plan a celebration (like a special meal or small gift)
   c. Put the person down

5. Your child is told a secret by a sibling. It's not about anything dangerous, but it is something the sibling doesn't want anyone else to know. Does your child:

   a. Tell you what was said in secret

   b. Keep the secret

   c. Tell the sibling, "You should tell Mom/Dad."

6. Your child's favorite piece of clothing is missing from his or her room. Your child:

   a. Crying and screaming, accuses others of taking it

   b. Asks if anyone knows where it is

   c. Shrugs and asks to buy another

   d. Cries, but won't tell anyone why

Section Two: Life at School

7. If there is a school election for class president, does your child:

   a. Think it's important

   b. Offer to run for the position or make known to others whom he or she supports

   c. Talk to you about the election campaign

   d. Ignore the election

8. A classmate of your child's calls to ask for the answers to the evening's homework. Your child:

   a. Gives the classmate the answers

   b. Tells the classmate to do the homework himself or herself

   c. Offers to help, and explains how the homework is done

9. A classmate is being teased at school about being a homosexual. Does your child:

   a. Tease the child, too

   b. Tell others to stop teasing him or her

   c. Tell you about the teasing

10. In your child's class at school, there is a boy with cerebral palsy who needs extra care. When the teacher asks for a volunteer to help him with his schoolwork, your child:

   a. Looks down and says nothing
   b. Makes jokes about the boy
   c. Volunteers

11. Your child is accused of being in a fight at school. Do you:
   a. Immediately blame the other child for starting the fight
   b. Doubt your child could ever get into a fight and believe that the school must be mistaken
   c. Punish your child without delving into who is really to blame
   d. Ask your child to explain what happened and expect him or her to accept the consequences

12. In school, if he or she needs help from a teacher, does your child:
   a. Ask the teacher for help
   b. Ask you to ask the teacher to help him or her
   c. Do nothing and fail or get poor grades

13. A group of children are excluding your child. Does your child:
   a. Threaten them
   b. Ignore them
   c. Ask you for advice
   d. Find other friends

14. If another child brought drugs or a weapon to school, would your child:
   a. Tell a teacher or administrator
   b. Tell you
   c. Tell the other child that this is dangerous
   d. Tell the other child how cool he or she is and say nothing about the drugs or weapon

15. At your child's school, when the staff plans events, is your child:
   a. Included in the decision-making process
   b. Told that these are decisions made by adults
   c. Allowed to make a token decision, something that students can decide but that is of little consequence to them

Section Three: Community Life

16. Your child is on a sports team or involved in another group activity with children who won't let him or her participate as often as the other children. Does your child:
    a. Stand up for his or her rights and tell the coach or leader
    b. Complain to you about the treatment
    c. Drop out

17. If your child is in trouble, will he or she:
    a. Trust a police officer for help
    b. Trust others besides you to help him or her
    c. Do nothing and let the situation get worse

18. How do others in your community see your child? Does your child hear he that or she is:
    a. Trustworthy
    b. A troublemaker
    c. Just like all other young people

19. If your son or daughter is being told he or she can't do something because of gender, does your child:
    a. Argue back and insist he or she get an opportunity to try
    b. Complain but do nothing
    c. Ask for help to change the rules that exclude him or her

20. Your child's aunt recently passed away from cancer. A fundraiser is planned in her honor. Does your child:
    a. Help organize the event
    b. Raise funds and participate
    c. Avoid doing anything
    d. Say he or she will raise some money, but never follow through on the promise

21. When your child gets angry at someone, does your child:
    a. Hurt the person
    b. Avoid the person
    c. Try to resolve the conflict

22. If people in your neighborhood hold an event, like a street party or a park cleanup, does your child:
   a. Avoid participating
   b. Tease others who participate
   c. Offer to help
   d. Do something to ruin the event

23. If someone gets hurt at the playground, does your child:
   a. Offer to get help from any adult who is available
   b. Laugh or ignore the accident
   c. Come and tell you about it later
   d. Feel upset, even cry about what he or she saw happen

24. If your child found a wallet on the street with fifty dollars in it, and no obvious identification, would your child:
   a. Keep the wallet hidden from everyone, even you
   b. Bring the wallet home and ask you to help find the owner
   c. Ask you to take him or her to the police station to turn it in

An answer key to help tally your child's score is at the back of the book.

The Security Cycle

Compassion, connection, responsibility, citizenship—this is the cycle we want to start at home. The alternative is selfishness, alienation, exploitation, and disenfranchisement. Big words to describe the loud-mouthed brats we meet who know nothing of their obligations to anyone else.

I hear frequently that today's kids don't respect their elders. When I talk to anxious parents on radio talk shows and in school gymnasiums, I am often told about a generation of rude and disrespectful young people. "They have no drive."

"They're irresponsible." "They do nothing for nobody but themselves." I won't disagree. But I also don't think we've understood why our children behave the way they do. Nor have we understood the profound influence parents and other adults have on how children behave. If we want our children to change their behavior, we will need to understand the part we play in making kids think Me instead of We.

Bob Marvin, a professor of psychology at the University of Virginia, and his colleagues have developed what they call the Circle of Security.[2] It is a simple concept to explain how very young children attach to their parents. But knowing how something is done and doing it are two very different things. Members of Marvin's research team present some compelling videos of young mothers and fathers working against the odds to raise their kids. Often themselves victims of neglect, these parents know little about how to make their children feel secure. In one video, a little girl is playing on the floor when her teenage mother enters the room. The little girl holds her arms out, to be picked up. Her mother walks by her, then smiles. She picks up a toy bus. Hands it to her child. The girl ignores the bus. Remains there on the floor, her arms now down at her side, her attention anywhere but with her mother.

Other tapes are even worse. A four-year-old stands at attention at her mother's side, eyes cast to the floor. Her mother is always angry, says her daughter never does anything she isn't told to do. The mother barks at her to sit down, and like a puppet, the girl squats. She hangs on her mother's every word. The little girl is doing anything she can to avoid calling attention to herself. Attention usually means a beating or, worse, a barrage of put-downs and name-calling. As she sits there on the floor, the little girl's face is expressionless. Her ears are attentive to her mother's commands, but her emotions are safely locked away.

How will either of these little girls ever parent her own son or daughter? How will she know how to cuddle her child? How will she help her son or daughter become a responsible citizen, someone who cares about the welfare of others? What will be her capacity to teach compassion? Though few parents are this dramatically abusive to their children, in our own ways we all run the risk of accidentally removing ourselves from our children's lives. If we want to keep our children connected, it is up to us to shape the world around them.

After all, if a child can't attract the attention of his parents by holding his arms up to them, then he can always be sure and get their attention by acting badly. For some children, provoking anger is simply a poorly conceived strategy to find a substitute for the hug they really want. As parents, we have the responsibility, no matter what our children do, to refrain from abusing them. Better, I think, that we try to understand what it is they want from us. Most likely it's our attention and, occasionally, some well-timed advice.

"But Will I Spoil Them?"

Of course, there are a few things that can go wrong. The most common complaint I hear from parents who are asked to show their children more compassion is that they worry they'll spoil them. Let's quickly put this fiction to rest. Parenting gurus from Dr. Spock to Penelope Leach all say the same thing: Babies can't be spoiled. Toddlers can't be held enough, if that's what they want. A teenager can never feel too much support. Mary Ainsworth, among the most influential theorists of child development, told Robert Karen, author of *Becoming Attached: First Relationships and How They Shape Our Capacity to Love*, that none of her research shows anything but positive benefits when parents provide warm, sensitive care to a child on demand. It does not create dependency. "It's a good thing," Ainsworth said, "to give a baby and a young child physical contact . . . especially when they want it and seek it. It doesn't spoil them. It doesn't make them clingy. It doesn't make them addicted to being held."[3]

The only real danger is when we inadvertently smother our children with our efforts to connect with them. While babies accept our swaddling, two-year-olds need permission to explore and the reassurance that they will receive our acceptance upon their return. When we smother them, insisting they come to us and "Give me a hug," we teach them that bigger people overpower little people. We show them how a bully acts. We force them into doing one of two things:

- *They can give in:* They can do what others tell them to do. They can stuff their feelings deep inside. Since they have not been shown compassion, they learn nothing about showing compassion to others. Most kids in this situation either grow up feeling guilty, insecure about their ability to please others, or angry and withdrawn. Either way, they know nothing of voluntarily making another person feel good. They know nothing about thinking genuine thoughts of We.

- *They can resist:* They can pull back. Have a tantrum. Refuse to participate. They can assert themselves and attack the parent who is smothering them. They can run away. These children, too, learn nothing about compassion or responsibility for others' feelings. In fact, as teens they are often out there, beyond our front doors, alone, and unattached to their parents at a time in their development when they could use some loving guidance. They are responsible for no one, but then, no one has acted responsibly toward them.

These children never experience the seeds of compassion that come from knowing we are valued by others for who we are.

Holding, handling, playing, mirroring back to a child the joy of her existence, all help to create in the child's mind an internal picture of how the world works. It is a scene that replays as she grows. It is what she expects to happen. The more chaotic a child's behavior, the more she needs a predictable world in which to grow.

The Push-Pull of Growing Up

Aiden has that predictable world. He is a rambunctious, easily distracted, and outgoing two-year-old. His mother and father are quick to tell you they like their little boy's outgoing character, but there are times when they just want a few moments of peace. In Aiden's little world, peace is only found when he's sleeping. Minute to minute, he navigates his surroundings. For a moment, he crawls up on his father's lap and then, all too quickly, he is back down on the ground, padding into the kitchen and climbing on the counters by working his way up the drawer handles. He is monkeylike in his explorations. He needs to be constantly watched.

But he always comes back to his father's or mother's lap. It's safe there. He explores and returns many times each day.

When his parents aren't there, gleefully welcoming him back to their knee each time, Aiden will go to anyone else who will look down at him and admire him. Each time Aiden finds someone, he learns a little more about how meaningful it is to be responded to. In fact, one could say that each time he finds an embrace, he is shown how to increase his own "response-ability."

It is a security cycle that winds like a tornado, lifting children from dependent little people up into the stratosphere of dependable adults. That cycle, whether for a two-year-old or a teenager, looks much the same. Each shouts in his or her own way, "I need you to support my discovery of the world." "I need you to watch over me." "Help me." "Delight in what I do." When the youngster tires or feels the need to share his experience, he finds his way back to a parent's knee (or kitchen table, where, over a midnight snack, a teenage version of the little boy will start talking about his life). The child who returns says to himself, "I need you to welcome me back." "I need you to protect me." "Comfort me." "Praise me." There, in our appreciative gaze, the child is also helped to organize his feelings. We can ask him, "Are you tired?" "Cold?" "Hungry?" Children, whether small or big, don't always have the words to describe how they are feeling.

"Do you need a hug, Honey?" Aiden's father asks when Aiden brushes by his knee for a second time, but coyly stays a foot or two out of reach. Aiden says nothing, but easily lets himself be lifted into the air. It's not long before hugs turn into squirms, and Aiden is down again and off with nary a backward glance.

At twelve, Aiden will still seek his father's attention. He'll ask to be driven to the mall, or he'll want to wrestle in the backyard. He'll leave his science project conspicuously on the kitchen counter, waiting for someone to see it. He'll want to talk at the most inopportune times. He'll yell only at his father and mother because he knows that only his parents' love will remain constant. With hormones flaring, that twelve-year-old will insist he be allowed to go to a class party. Aiden's parents will be anxious about his going to the home where they don't know the parents. Their car will be inconveniently in the shop. Aiden will have to take a bus to get there. Some other parents will call to say they'll drive him home. It will be hard to let him go, but he will look so certain that this is what he wants. He will be as determined then as he was at age two. His parents will stop and think about the situation as Aiden is experiencing it. They will see how much he is still their little boy, anxious to explore: an adventure seeker. They will, as they must, reluctantly agree to let him continue his adventures.

When Aiden returns that evening, he will have a story to tell. He will set himself down at the foot of his parents' bed. It's not quite his father's knee, but it will be close. He will know he's safe there. He will want to impress his parents with how well he coped. He will tell them all about a noisy bus ride and the driver having to tell some kids to behave themselves. About a party where two boys went outside and smoked. About the more precocious of his friends slinking off to kiss in a back room.

Aiden's parents will smile and nod, but won't ask too many questions. When they have all the facts, Aiden's father will ask his son, "How did it all feel? For you?"

"I dunno," Aiden might answer.

"Scary? Or did you feel like you could handle it?"

"It was okay. I didn't go into the back bedrooms, though."

Aiden will do these things over and over again. He'll test his parents' capacity for compassion, just as he did as a toddler. He'll keep trying to be more responsible for himself because he has their support. He will keep trying to measure up to the standards they have set. After all, they're the ones he really wants to impress.

When all is said and done, Aiden will be convinced that they really care about his personal welfare. He'll feel the attunement that comes with years of dancing his way to maturity in a home where responsibility and expectations are the musical accompaniment. He'll want to impress his parents now and for always. He'll want to act just like them. He'll want to grow to be just as capable of caring for others as they have shown themselves to be capable of caring for him.

The Neglected Child

Not all children are so fortunate. Generations of Native North American children were forcibly taken from their parents. The same thing happened in Australia. Those who took the children from their families to put them into heartless, even abusive, boarding schools thought it was their God-given right to "civilize" these children. Civilizing them meant beating them when they spoke their native language. It meant that many children never felt the warmth of any adult's touch for months, often years.

That's what cultural genocide looks like. It twists individual children's sense of compassion for others and for themselves. Far from civilizing, it simply destroys the very heart of caring and responsibility, which are the cornerstones of civil society. One needs to ask, Who were the real barbarians? How could they do that to children?

If we can understand the pain imposed on Native people, we might glimpse the far, far lesser pain we are causing other young people. What we can learn from the horrific experiences of Native people is that when children are denied the love of a parent, or a grandparent, foster parent, or other substitute caregiver, the map inside their heads of how the world is supposed to be takes on ominous shadings. The terrain looks dangerous. They stop expecting to ever find a knee to climb on.

Without the experience of compassion being shown to us, the notion of ourselves as loving beings remains shrouded. It is only a short step from abandonment to pain—physical, emotional, and spiritual. In pain, we will do whatever we can to go numb: drugs, alcohol, suicide . . . long hours at the office, compulsive sex, endless travel that helps us avoid establishing connections with anyone. All are possible escapes for people who never felt another's unconditional love.

These ways of coping also avoid responsibility. Even the workaholic isn't necessarily demonstrating responsibility to others. Motivated by personal gain and using time at the office to avoid intimacy, the workaholic uses work as another way to avoid thinking about what the person really needs or what others need from him or her.

Roots and Wings

Give a child both roots and wings, and you will raise a child who understands the needs of others. Like Aiden, children need a secure harbor from which to explore and the safety of a breakwater to shelter them when they put back into port. They need to know the world is predictable and safe and that it's a place they can assert themselves without too many consequences. It's easy to teach this when we travel with our children. Not to amusement parks or structured camp-grounds. I'm talking about showing our children a world of adventure that can be found through a visit to a large city and letting them wander a bit on their own (if they're old enough to handle it) or a back-country extreme holiday that involves challenge and sweat. In both cases, the adventure we place in front of our kids is going to help them grow strong. When we coach them well on how to navigate the dangers they'll face, even if we simply advise them to listen to their instructors and wear their safety equipment, they are going to launch into the world with confidence in their ability to look after themselves and be depended on by others. They will learn responsibility.

Adventures like that are designed by parents. They don't just happen.

If we are there at the other end of the adventure, ready to hear all about it, we are giving our children the predictability that fosters an optimistic attitude toward life. We are letting them educate us (and themselves) about how competent they really are. That's a gift we give our children that is every bit as poignant as our love. We give them a sense of themselves as capable. This sense of capability, and the gift of love, aren't so distant from one another.

Of course, launching our kids is not about our abdicating our common sense or our boundaries. If two-year-old Aiden is climbing next to the stove, then obviously, we'll need to do two things. First, we'll need to block the kitchen entrance to keep him safe. Second, we'll need to take him to the monkey bars at the park and let him climb as high as he wants. Simply standing in the kitchen yelling at the poor boy, "Stop climbing!" tells him that he is wrong. Everything about him is wrong and what he is driven to do is wrong. Those messages leave emotional scars.

The twelve-year-old who has always been told "No," "Stop," "Wait," "Don't," and even "Abstain," all his life knows nothing about himself or how to self-regulate. He knows nothing of others trying to understand his needs. He has never experienced others acting responsibly toward him. Sure, they've kept him protected, but they haven't shown him compassion for his feelings. They haven't modeled how to be responsible for another's well-being.

We seldom get it right as parents. Thankfully, our kids are forgiving. Even if they storm out on us, or yell. Even if we have to remind them tersely that such behavior is unacceptable, no matter what they're feeling. Even if we have to say no more often than yes (and we want to say "Yes!" much more often)—even then, our children will know that we love them if they are confident that we are waiting for their return.

Face-to-Face

I'm talking here about something quite old-fashioned. Touch. Embraces. Face-to-face conversation. Our children today enjoy a great advantage that comes with global connections. All that wired and wireless media can broaden their understanding of the world and make boundaries and borders evaporate. But whether all that becomes of any use to our children will depend on their very real connections with the people around them. Their ethical conduct in our homes, schools, and communities, and on the Web, is still something they learn from their parents and other caregivers.

It can seem these days that we've mistaken the roots of empathy for simple interaction. As I'll show in Chapter 5, being next to someone is not necessarily the same as being connected, spiritually, physically, or emotionally. Why, we might wonder, do our children seek connections in the wrong way?

- A thirteen-year-old girl dates a nineteen-year-old boy. Her parents wonder why. Maybe because the touch and commitment she seeks is to be found in his arms. Maybe she finds there a sense of her as responsible, older. Something powerful to say about herself may come from being on his motorcycle, or even in his bed. She is not likely to be looking for danger and early pregnancy. But when connections and responsibility are in short supply elsewhere, older boyfriends and early initiation into sex can be a poor second choice.

- A fourteen-year-old boy steals a car and takes his friends for a joy ride. His parents wonder why. Maybe it's because he wants to feel like he's older. Maybe he wants to feel that others look at him and admire him. Maybe he wants someone to tell him how cool (i.e., important) he is. There is an awful rush of responsibility that comes with acting so recklessly. As odd as that sounds, young people themselves associate responsibility with such senseless rites of passage as stealing cars, using drugs, early sexual initiation, and even going to jail. These are ways they feel the embrace of their peers, the warmth of recognition for a fledgling status as adult.

Our children want to be touched, physically and emotionally.

They want to experience trust.

They want opportunities to act responsibly.

The three flow together. The child who feels attached to her family will have a better chance of experiencing empathy for others as a consequence of its being shown to her. The child who feels embraced and then is given opportunities to act independent of her parents will understand what it means to be trusted. Like the toddler who is left for a moment on the slide to navigate her way up to the top and back down again, an older child learns compassion and responsibility through teachable moments. Parents teach their children by filling spaces with love and by leaving spaces for children to take responsibility. Through the experience of many such moments, we convey the messages "I trust you" and "I know you can do this."

Acting responsibly follows naturally. If I feel compassion extended to me and trusted in my abilities to exercise some say over my life, then I will give something back to others. After all, I want others to be there to watch me. I can only know I'm worth something if I'm acknowledged by others. They are my audience. So I act responsibly to get their applause. I show compassion because it feels good, and mimic what I have been taught. I know trust because I have been trusted. I show respect for others because I understand what it feels like to be shown respect.

Acting responsibly is a way we demonstrate the strength of our connections. It sews us into the fabric of our family and community. The more a child knows about the lived experiences of others, the more that child identifies these others as being just like her. Meet a child face-to-face in Egypt, and suddenly the plight of Middle Eastern children is not so abstract. Indeed, the child now knows that her life and that of others are a jumble of intersecting interests.

Give that child the tools to act responsibly, and she will. She will say to herself, "I'm here" and "I count."

Tips List

There are many ways to encourage children to think and act responsibly. In most cases, they are learning from the adults in their lives how to be a responsible citizen. Here are some suggestions from families that I know are trying to show their children what is expected of them.

- Tell your children you expect them to do things for others, not just for themselves.
- Insist that children show respect to their teachers, coaches, and other elders who make an effort to make children's lives better. Being clear in your expectations makes it easier for children to understand how to behave properly.
- Avoid always being ready and willing to do things for your children. Leave space for them to ask you for help and to initiate their own solutions to their problems.
- Encourage your child to join a team. Be sure to talk with your child about team dynamics and how he or she can be part of a group without becoming a part of destructive cliques.
- If your child has the talent, encourage him or her to join a youth orchestra. Your child will quickly learn, "If I don't practice my part, no one succeeds."
- Ask your child to bicycle to the store to pick up some milk (bicycle with him or her if the child is too young to go alone).
- Encourage siblings to sort out their own problems and to spend time with each other (travel as a family, but turn off the DVD player and electronic gaming console in the car so family members can talk with one another).
- Help at a homeless shelter to better appreciate the challenges other families face.
- Volunteer in another community with those who are disadvantaged (refugees, victims of a natural disaster, etc.). Leaving our own community helps our children understand diversity and tolerance.

- Help put up posters for a lost cat or a community event.
- Stop sheltering your older children from the truth about their family, community, or school. Instead, as they grow old enough to understand, introduce them to the bigger problems people face when they live together.
- Encourage children to make decisions that they can make for themselves.
- Give your child a watch and an alarm clock, and then let him suffer the consequences of being late.
- Ask your children to help you shop, and then let them make their own lunches.
- Sign a contract about drinking and driving with your older teens. Be clear about what is expected of them, but be ready to bail them out of a situation the first time they make a mistake.
- Ensure there are logical consequences to things children do that harm themselves or others. Make those consequences direct and meaningful.
- Set boundaries that are respectful of what is a child's own business and what is the entire family's business and concern.
- Don't give children everything they want (but most of what they need).

chapter **three**

Adult Mirrors, Adult Mentors

A We Generation doesn't just spontaneously sprout among cell phones and Internet chatter. It is nurtured into being through the everyday, one-to-one connections our children experience with parents and mentors at home and school. If children are to take full advantage of their electronic connections, to become the first generation ever that can truly think and act globally, they are going to first need to experience the warmth of fleshy connections. It is these first connections that lay the foundation stones for compassion.

I am an optimist. I see in the virtual world we are creating the potential for our children to become the most attuned, compassionate generation ever. They understand the world as a place without borders. Such a world was beautifully described by Commander William C. McCool, who died aboard the space shuttle Columbia in 2003. He said from space, "From our orbital vantage point, we observe an earth without borders, full of peace, beauty and magnificence, and we pray that humanity as a whole can imagine a borderless world as we see it, and strive to live as one in peace." As simplistic as it may sound, the capacity of our children to make good on the promise of a borderless world starts with how we and our children interact. Parents need to give children the space to explore and a safe harbor to return to so that they may feel secure in the very large room we call our Earth.

Perhaps parenting is like aikido, one of the Japanese defensive martial arts. Sometimes used to train people to protect themselves against family violence, aikido teaches balance. As my colleague Sombat Tapanya, a psychologist and aikido master in Thailand, explained to me, it is always better "giving in to get your way." Aikido teaches its students to work with another's force, redirecting it toward the defender's goal. Holding our children close against their wishes will only cause strife. Allowing them space to leave us tells them it is safe to return without threat of being smothered.

In this increasingly complex world of connected kids, their first connections with those at home are still so important to their growing into responsible adults.

Even as they leave us, they are always looking backward. Young people like Christina, whose story was told in the introduction, want parents, teachers, coaches, grandparents, the police, store clerks, bus drivers, and just about everyone else in their community to notice them. These youngsters certainly make a point of it, too. All that noise they make with their hair, clothing, piercings, and music. How can we help but pay attention?

When we capture them in our gaze, our compassion pays forward. The more we show it to our kids, the more it multiplies as they show it to others. Our little one cries after a fall from the monkey bars, and we kiss the "booboo" but know the real injury is to our child's fledgling narcissism. Our real work is to heal the emotional wound, to reassure our child that she is still whole, competent, independent. Psychoanalyst Heinz Kohut taught us that these small failures threaten our children's sense of self-importance.[1] For a moment, it is as if they shatter. The good news is that there, under a parent's gaze, they can do better than Humpty Dumpty. They can pull themselves back together again.

In such instances, the smallest of embraces teaches kids the biggest of lessons. The compassion shown to them makes them receptive to others' discomfort. It is not unusual to see a small child mimicking a parent, soothing a younger sibling, a pet, or a doll, cooing softly at the loved one, rocking the hurt away.

Grandparents Offer Grand Connections

Grandparents are the most versatile of resources. They have all the elements of the perfect adult: They have the time to pay attention to their grandkids. They have stories to tell (our kids love to hear people tell them stories, not as lectures, but as tales of adventure, near misses, brushes with disaster). And in most cases, their grandchildren matter to them.

Anyone who has seen the Academy Award–winning movie *Little Miss Sunshine* will know what I mean. Alan Arkin plays the grandfather in this quirky comedy about family life. His granddaughter has his undivided attention as she prepares for a children's beauty pageant. Even after his death, there is still continuity in Arkin's attachment with the girl. He is still joyfully present at the pageant, as unbelievably boisterous as ever. There is a good lesson to be learned from the film: What grandparents share with their grandchildren lingers.

It's odd how we can hear from our grandparents truths or advice that we refuse to hear from our parents. We can appreciate their wisdom, probably because they have no real power to tell us what to do. They rule through their moral authority alone. I can certainly recall long conversations with the one grandparent I knew, my grandmother. Even as a little boy, I loved her outspoken criticism of others, the way her arthritic hands still managed to knit me new socks and mittens every November. I liked it when she told me secrets about my mother that made my mother seem more vulnerable. The older I got, the more I appreciated the ally I had in her. When she died, a swift death following a diagnosis of bone cancer that helped explain her tiredness, she left me with an enduring sense that I mattered. She understood and respected that I had an opinion, and she made me feel that in time, it would count.

Her memory reminds me to offer my own children an ally that isn't me.

Children need lots of kinds of relationships. They need to huddle in secret and giggle at authority. "Here you go," my grandmother would say, and slip me a candy before dinner from the silver tin she kept beside her recliner. It would be our secret. It was a relationship I could navigate without my parents. It was a safe place to learn about what it meant to be treated compassionately and to compassionately treat another. There were small chores to do for my grandmother. She always seemed to need someone to stand in front of her, hands out, so she could roll a skein of wool. There was food to bring her and dishes to take back to the kitchen. There

were problems with her television's rabbit ears to fix and pil-
lows to be adjusted. Looking back, I wonder if she was just
trying to find ways to make me feel useful. Were all the little
chores just a way of her prolonging our time together? The
thought warms me.

Big-Kid Strategies for Connecting

Teens are no different, just bigger and ungainly. Your son
comes back from a date, surly and slamming doors for no
good reason. Or so it seems. Soon his music is blaring and he
won't turn it down, no matter how loud you shout.

Try dropping your voice. Gently knock on his door. Wait.
Think of your time as something you can offer to soothe a
very bruised ego. Think of your presence like a coo, your
pacing of the love you will show as measured as it was the
first time you spoke to your child outside the womb.

Your teenage son may or may not have much to say about
what happened. But a little gentleness, coupled with your in-
sistence the music be turned down, might just get you a qui-
eter house and insight into his emotional maelstrom. There
are lots of ways we can show tenderness at such moments.
By offering a snack (food and teens work wonderfully together) and a little impromptu conversation.

If you don't get the response you're hoping for, don't
think it was wasted effort or that you've somehow spoiled
him by not arguing with him over his rude behavior. After
all, kids shouldn't be allowed to slam doors. But save those
battles for later, when everyone is calmer.

Meanwhile, pat yourself on the back. You have just given
your son a more valuable lesson. Your son has looked into
your face and seen how much he counts. He has sensed you

understand, even if just superficially, his discomfort. You've modeled for him how to handle an emotional crisis. And you've prepared him to help someone else do the same.

There is a formula here.

The three Ts: time, touch, talk

If I've learned anything from the many children and families I've spoken with, it is that we nurture in our children a sense of connectedness through some very simple means. By offering them our time, our touch, and our talk.

Time

Our young people need both quality and quantity in the time they spend with us. If they come home every day to an empty house, spend every lunch hour alone in front of a television, or really only ever share their lives with us for ten days of stressful vacation time each year (and most of that in an amusement park or a campground), then we are going to have trouble hearing the spontaneous.

Quality time happens because quantity time is made available.

Be there for your kids, and they will share. Just be prepared to turn down the television, take a pot off the stove, hang up the phone, and turn your back on your own computer when they do. That's if you're lucky enough to catch them during daylight hours.

Teenagers seem to love the wee hours of the morning to skulk into our bedrooms and tell us everything that is so important and can't wait until morning. As inconvenient as it might be, the concerned parent who is available (can be reached) and accessible (is really listening) will teach a child much about how we show that we value someone else.

Touch

This T needs a whole chapter. Chapter 5 will discuss touch at length. But for now, in brief, let me explain that I'm not just talking about physical hugs and kisses. Touch is about intentional communication. It is about fixing our gaze on our children and letting them know they matter. It is about sensing their upset before the tears well. And it is about offering a knee, a hand to hold, a hug, a gesture of caring in tune with what the child wants.

Talk

If we provide the time, and the touch, the talk will follow. Many parents worry that all those programmed activities our kids attend are destroying family life. Uh-huh. Think back to when you were growing up. Did you and your parents speak often? Did they really know what you were feeling? How much time and how much touch were you offered? It's easy to mythologize the past, telling tall tales of epic love. It might even be true. But we revel in the past at the risk of overlooking what we have to work with today.

Those long car rides to soccer practice in rush-hour traffic (my kids always seemed to play at five-thirty on a Wednesday evening) are a time, eyes forward, when talk is easy. Breezy. Simple or profound. From the child's point of view, it's perfect. Her parent has already taken the time to be there for her, even if it is "just a drive." In the isolation of the car, there is an intensity, a psychic touch. "I'm here for you, right now," is the message. Don't be shy to gently turn the conversation to what she did at school. Ask her to tell you about her friends. Ask her what it's like to be on a team and what she thinks their chances are of getting to the playoffs.

Don't lecture.

Don't use that time to tell her what you think she should do.

Don't use that time to tell her how to play her sport.

Don't use that time to criticize—not her friends, clothing, or music.

If you run out of things to ask her about, you can always model for her how to share by treating her to a sneak preview of what it means to be an adult.

Tell her about your day.

Tell her about the challenges you face at work, at home, and with the neighbors.

The better we show our children the three Ts, the better they will be at showing them to others. My wife caught my son, now a young teen, on the phone with his girlfriend. They usually text or instant-message one another, but that evening they were actually talking. Or at least his girlfriend was. Cathy watched him as he remained on the computer, doing his homework, gaming, chatting, and God only knows what else, occasionally saying "Uh-huh," or "Yeah," while the poor girl kept talking.

Later, after he had hung up, Cathy sat him down and explained to him something about girls. "We like to talk," she said. "And we deserve more respect than that, don't you think?" He sheepishly nodded. "It's okay to say you're busy, and ask to talk later or in school tomorrow, but to not pay attention, that's not being a gentleman, or a friend. It's just rude."

Later Cathy and I chuckled. As John Gray, the celebrated couple's counselor, has explained, men may be from Mars and women from Venus, but that doesn't mean we can't figure out how to respect each other's differences. The truth is that both sexes want each other's time, touch, and talk. Only it gets expressed in different ways. It's up to us adults to help our kids learn how to give of themselves to others. That's a lesson we are eminently qualified to teach.

Empathy

Mary Gordon has made it her life's work to awaken in young people an understanding of empathy.[2] The Roots of Empathy is an experiential education program that brings a neighborhood infant and parent into an elementary-school or a junior-high classroom once every three weeks for a year. Program instructors invite students to watch the baby's development and understand the child's feelings. It is experiential learning in which the baby is the "teacher." It is an effective program that helps teach kids emotional literacy. The result is schools that are safer, more empathic places for kids to interact with one another.

Gordon tells the story of a fourteen-year-old boy who had been abandoned at age four when his mother was murdered. He went from foster home to foster home after that, becoming tougher and tougher with each move. He was a menace who was best kept respectfully at a distance. She was surprised, of course, when he donned the Snugli baby carrier and took the baby in his arms from its mother, nestling it close to his chest. "Then this big boy went off into the corner and he rocked back and forth with the baby, hugging it in the Snugli. When he came back a few minutes later, he took the baby out very gently, and gave the baby back to the Mom, and then he said to our instructor, 'Do you think that if no one ever loved you, you could still be a good father?'"[3]

There are many opportunities that can be found to nurture our children's development of empathy for others, even in the midst of a period of great pain and dysfunction. It's not just parents who can help, though as parents, we play a profound role in jump-starting the process. When we're not available, our kids can call for roadside service to get a boost when their emotional batteries go dead. At least, they can if they know what number to call and that the service is available. At such times, other adults can play the roles of mirrors and mentors. Mirrors are people who reflect back to our children their importance. Mentors show our children how to be their best. From a school instructor to the parent of a friend, all adults have the potential to be significant in the lives of children other than their own.

The roots of empathy are in the small embraces our children find in their classrooms; on their playgrounds; at recreation centers, sports clubs, and swimming lessons; and even in how they are treated when they buy a hot chocolate at the mall.

From Continuity Grows Attachment

A short while ago, I saw such small embraces working their magic in a part of India known more for violence than for Gandhi-like pacifism. Imphal is a small city on the east side of Bangladesh, snuggled next to Burma and Bhutan. If you can't quite picture it, you're not alone. It is a remote place, even by India's standards. It is also a place few Westerners can go. An ethnic war for independence has raged for decades. More than two hundred local tribal groups want their independence from India and are willing to die demanding it. Arms and insurgents flow liberally across the adjacent borders. What resources India gives to the region come more often in the shape of soldiers, tanks, and police stations rather than schools and sewage systems. There is poverty in a land that looks postcard-pretty when the fields are planted and you forget that the roads have deteriorated into muddy sluices.

Much of the social safety net is provided through aid organizations, including the churches. The only real schools preparing children for the future are those where priests and nuns teach. The public schools are rife with patronage. Underqualified teachers teach little or nothing during the day and instead charge parents a fee to tutor their children in the evening. Year-end exams determine a child's future. Fail, and doors to higher education slam shut.

Amid this chaos, a growing number of young people cope by using drugs. An increasing number of women, in particular, are becoming heroin addicts. On the outskirts of Imphal is a church-sponsored shelter for these women. It is a place for them to kick their habit. It is also a place where they can learn a craft, plant a small garden, and pocket a few dollars to start a home business when they are ready to leave. While the nuns' efforts at the shelter would be noteworthy on their own, what caught my attention was what they do for the children. Every woman who comes to the shelter is encouraged to bring her children. Best of all, the children attend, at no charge, one of the finest schools in the city, which is run by the same order of nuns. I was impressed. But I was even more impressed when I learned that if a child's mother relapses, leaves the shelter, and goes back to heroin and the violence and prostitution that go with it, the children can stay. The nuns make space for them. The kids continue their schooling. They continue to live with the hope of a better future. The doors to the shelter remain open to their mother.

I know of few places in the West that do so much for families. In most cases where children live with their mother at a shelter, a mother's relapse means a disruption in the children's care. They are evicted, most likely into foster homes, sometimes to relatives. That they may want to stay and be with the people who have proven their worth as caregivers matters little. There is no place at these inns; the children must leave.

What I saw in India reminded me that continuity in care is needed to inspire compassion in a child. Like a wire strung between two poles, the present and the future, a child needs to know that the relationship he or she starts will continue for some time to come. It is parents, and a community of other concerned adults, who provide this much-needed bonding over time. Creating that continuity with kids is possible, no matter how mad our lives seem. Even when we parents are in crisis, others can pinch-hit for us.

Here are a few successful ways parents I know have conveyed the message to their kids over time that they matter. Even when a parent can't physically be there, he or she can still use techniques to make a kid feel connected:

1. Extended family, including grandparents, are often a sure bet when it comes to creating continuity: Teenagers often appear for a time to have more in common with their strange uncle, eccentric aunt, or curmudgeonly grandfather. Suddenly, these colorful characters may offer your child a powerful ally as she tries to figure out who she wants to be when she grows up.

Try the following:

- *Send your kids packing—for a visit to a relative.* These trips can turn the heat down; extended family is great when parents and kids need a short break from each other. Not only does a visit ease tensions, but it also conveys to kids they are still part of a family that cares about them. The sage advice of an uncle or aunt might be easier to hear than a warning from a parent.

- *Encourage strange encounters.* Encourage your kids to have contact with relatives who are quite different from you. What your child learns about tolerance will serve her well later.

- *Don't be shy with the stories.* All those crazy childhood experiences you had with your siblings are worth retelling. They are a way of making children feel they are part of a larger family with its own unique history.

2. Neighbors, family friends, and other children's parents can make children feel they belong. These days, we all tend to be so busy. Relying on other adults in our communities makes sense if we want to give our children a sense of belonging. It is very much like placing your child in the middle of a hall of mirrors. In every direction he looks, he sees something different about himself reflected back. For my son, this means that with Mr. Bogada next door, he is a silly, reckless boy-adventurer whose game of tag with his buddies accidentally trampled Mr. Bogada's tomatoes. My son's teammate's mother, who drives him and two other kids to indoor soccer on weekends, sees him as a mature young man. She has a quirky taste in music and loves iced cappuccinos, which she is happy to buy for all the boys when they come back from the gym so sweaty she has to drive with the windows down

and the defrost blowing. Then there's Salim, who tends the counter at the corner store. He's a surly old man when kids misbehave in his store, but if they are polite, he is quick to forgo pennies. He seems never to get right the number of candies that my son buys in brown paper bags. There are always more than a few extra for the fifty cents my son has spent. If we look around our communities, our children experience a web of connections that hold them firmly in place. The people who create these connections with them come in many shapes and sizes. Though occasionally we meet someone we wish our children would avoid, for the most part I've found the connections our children make add to their lives. These connections should not be overlooked.

Try the following:

- *Encourage children to talk to strangers.* Okay, not strangers who are so strange that we can't keep track of them. But encouraging our kids to be out in their communities is a great way to make them feel they belong. Teach them to say hello to people, waitresses, bus drivers, and new neighbors out walking their dogs, or elderly people out on their front porches. Show children how to foster community.
- *Encourage them to deal with problems.* As crises occur in their lives or in the lives of their friends, use these teachable moments to talk about proper behavior when one lives in a community. What should they do if friends are shoplifting? What should they do if other kids are cutting through people's gardens? How should they handle someone speaking rudely to them? The more we prepare our kids to be responsible members of their communities, the more neighborliness they will find.

- *Share responsibility.* Offering to be a support to other kids makes it more likely other parents will support our kids. Most parents love a house full of kids. Most moms or dads gladly drive a carload of kids to games or birthday parties. The more we extend ourselves, the more likely our own kids will have favors extended to them.

- *Help children find a place in their community.* The best way to become a part of a community is to participate. The more our kids find their own place doing volunteer work such as mowing lawns or fund-raising, or doing odd jobs, and the more they know their neighbors and are responsible for their actions, the more our children will feel a part of a community that values them.

3. Schools are more than places of learning: Schools are our children's second homes. Who among us didn't fall in love with the grade four teacher (or was it grade two, or grade five?), been shocked by the lunacy of the adult who taught English in grade seven (or was it social studies in grade nine? Math in grade ten?). I often think our value as adults is to broaden children's horizons, to offer them a sense of what can be, not just what is. Schools provide such intense relationships that they can't help but influence. When they help, they help a lot. When they fail, they hurt for a long time. And no wonder. Schools provide a continuity of attachment. Day in and day out, our children interact with their educators, school support staff, teaching assistants. Over time, these special individuals help our child figure out who she is. What these others see, our child comes to see about herself. In fact, among the best predictors of a child's academic success are the expectations of her teachers.[4] Teachers play an important role in nurturing a child's attitude toward success over time.

Shown compassion and offered responsibility, our children can grow at school into We-thinkers.

Try the following:

- *Encourage your child to stay after school.* Encourage your son to get involved in the extracurricular activities at his school and to create healthy relationships with the adults there. To clean the chalkboard or the whiteboard—okay, so that may be a bit old-fashioned, but the more we encourage our children to participate in the school and take responsibility for seeing that the school runs well, the better they will be at showing compassion and exercising responsibility. Student council? Recycling projects? Class monitors? School concerts? In every school, there are ways our children can participate and feel a part of the lives of others.

- *Make it possible for your child to follow her passion.* Most teachers and support staff are happy to extend themselves a little further when a child shows interest. Whatever your child loves to do, whether it is playing chess or dodgeball, encourage her to let her teachers know. Not only will she receive validation, but she's also more likely to tap hidden resources. Who knew that Mr. MacGuigan, your daughter's sixth-grade teacher, enjoys a game of chess at lunch, or that Ms. Currie, the vice principal, is happy to open the gym at recess once a week for an impromptu basketball game?

In the landscape of human contact, there can be many places for a child to feel the shelter of others. Looking up into our faces, children find reassurance of their self-worth. Our eyes are a place they find out how much they count; our attention, an opportunity to be shown how to make others feel important. It doesn't always work, mind you, but it works often enough to make me confident about the merits of creating communities of compassionate adults. Such communities will play a pivotal role nurturing the members of a We Generation, so that they give a damn about the communities from which they come.

The End of Ever After

We haven't been very good at modeling for our children stick-to-itiveness. We flit from relationship to relationship. Pro hockey players do it with their team allegiances. It's the same in most other sports as well. I find it difficult to get very excited about any city team these days. It seems the only thing that distinguishes one from the other is the amount of money they have to buy the talent. It is hard to feel pride when this year's stars can be traded away in the off-season. What makes our team more special than any other? A different-colored jersey—not much else.

So much for fidelity or commitment. The myth of happily ever after died a long time ago. I'm not just talking about marriage. While I can understand the attraction to a more temperate clime, I'm baffled when grandparents who retire move to some nameless community in the desert, leaving behind their children, grandchildren, and community. I'm just as confused by people's migration away from friends for jobs that bring a little more money but lots more anonymity. Behaviors like these are a problem if our goal is to teach children to be responsible for others. Children need connections, and connections take time to solidify. Those kids in the women's shelter in Imphal, India, are not just getting an education. They are being reminded they count and that to-morrow is predictable.

It needn't be "forever" to have an impact. While impul-sive shifts in loyalties don't do our children any good (nor our sports teams), a divorce isn't necessarily going to mean your kids turn into delinquents, either. I've actually coun-seled parents on occasion to get divorced when the tension in the home was making life worse for the kids. Whether their parents are divorced or married, children tell me the conti-nuity they seek comes in many flavors. In truth, for some kids, after a divorce they actually feel as though they get more undivided attention from their parents. If they are moving back and forth between two caring adults, one week on, one week off, there may be more energy for the kids and less for fighting.

Divorce Needn't Cause Trauma

No wonder divorce poses only a small threat to the well-being of children. If, for example, we look at the mental health of kids from homes where there has been no divorce, 90 percent are likely to be doing fine and need no profes-sional help. Among families where there has been a divorce, 80 percent still do just fine.[5] And that, despite the frequent tumbles into poverty divorced families sometimes experi-ence. What we have forgotten in the hyperbole of those who would preserve families at any cost is that children can show remarkable resilience when it comes to temporary separa-tions with their parents. A child who knows that a parent's love is unconditional is not likely to experience a divorce as deeply traumatic. A short period of absence needn't cause distress when there is the certainty of reconnection.

What does cause children stress is when they feel abandoned. When a father (as happens most often) or a mother uses the divorce as an excuse to absent himself or herself from a child's life, then the emotional scar is deep and festering. Our jails are full of abandoned or neglected children who grew into little tyrants. When both parents keep a relationship with their kids and shelve their disagreements to get on with the business of parenting, there is less likely to be any negative impact on the children. There's seldom anything fickle about such transitions. Families are not hockey teams. Most of the parents I've met who made the decision to "switch teams" did so only after a great deal of soul-searching.

When Divorce Hurts, It Hurts Bad

Grant and Connor knew their parents, Trish and Clarence, had to break up long before it happened. The boys are twelve and fifteen now. It's been five years since they lived with their two parents together, and their parents' arguing. Not that everything has improved since. Trish struggles to support the three of them by working two jobs. Clarence used to help out a little when he lived near enough that the boys could go visit. If they visited. When Clarence remarried, his new wife, Jeanie, found the boys too unruly, too much like Clarence's ex-wife, to let them alone when they were in her space. There were lots and lots of rules: where the boys could play, which rooms were off-limits, how to set the table.

Once, when Connor talked back, Jeanie sent him to his room without dinner. Clarence said nothing. He figured the boy had it coming and blamed Trish for not raising her sons properly. Still, he made sure his home was always just a little better at providing for the boys than Trish's. He bought the boys each his own iPod, though they weren't allowed to take them to their mother's. He even got Grant his own dog, a perky terrier pup that arrived Christmas Day. Grant named it Snitch. For a while, the gifts worked. As bad as Jeanie was, the boys felt that their father loved them.

Things got a lot worse when Clarence and Jeanie had their own child, a girl, two years after Trish and Clarence's divorce. Jeanie moved the baby into Grant's room and moved him in with Connor. Suddenly, Grant and Connor weren't allowed to come over so often on Sundays. The puppy, their iPods, all remained at their father's.

It all came to a head two years before I met the boys. Connor had had enough and refused to visit at all. Grant blew up at Jeanie and accused her of separating the family. He threatened to kill the baby. He said he was taking his dog to his mother's house. Clarence slapped him and sent him back to Trish. The father refused to see Grant for a month. After that, Grant visited alone, but only for a few hours at a time. He refused to speak to Jeanie. Six months later, Clarence told Grant that he and Jeanie and the baby were moving to the Middle East. He was going to work as part of a security team protecting foreign nationals. He said it wasn't as dangerous as it sounded.

"Can I take Snitch to Mom's?" Grant asked his father.

"We'll see," his father said.

Grant hasn't seen his father since. Trish brought the boys in for counseling when problems at home kept ending in yelling matches. The sound of her sons' voices—like those of grown men now—screaming at her reminded her of her time with Clarence. She thought she'd raised her sons better. She cried heavy tears that wet the front of her blouse each time we met. When that happened, Grant and Connor sat quietly, occasionally poking at each other, sometimes remembering to pass their mother a tissue from the box I keep on a table in my meeting room.

It took three months to get Grant to speak about what had happened with his father. There was a lot to get through first. Grant wasn't going to school as often as he should. His mother kept getting calls at work about him. After school, rather than coming home and doing his homework as he'd been told, he went and hung out at a friend's place nearby, watched television, or went to the mall. Everything seemed to be going wrong. When Grant's school held a fund-raiser for a school trip, he took home two boxes of chocolate bars to sell and then promptly gave them away to his friends or ate them himself. When it came time to hand in the sixty dollars he owed, he had shrugged and said he didn't have it. Trish paid the school, but knew something was desperately wrong with her son. The money came out of her Christmas fund. She had no idea how she was now going to afford the new iPods her sons wanted.

Maybe it was his embarrassment about the chocolate bars, or maybe it was finally realizing how hard his mother was trying, but Grant finally broke down and cried during one of our meetings. It was a door opener.

"It must be difficult for you," I said, "not knowing where your father is. Or your dog."

I had guessed that Grant wasn't likely to tell me much yet about how he felt about his dad, but I was willing to bet he was ready to speak about Snitch. The dog's disappearance had hung in the room like a silent predator waiting to be noticed.

"He gave the dog to the pound," Grant said. Trish nodded. She'd had an e-mail from Clarence six weeks after he'd left. She'd told Grant a few weeks later what had happened. Grant sniffled. His mother handed him a tissue, leaned closer toward him and touched his shoulder. "Why did he do that?" Grant cried. "We would have taken him. I told him that. I told him!"

I've heard lots of stories of loss during my career and met lots of abused children who carry the scars of neglect and violence, but there was something about Clarence's selfishness that made my eyes moisten. How could he do that? I wondered silently to myself. How could anyone do something so senseless and mean?

It would take some time, but eventually we helped Grant experience some more authentic attachments. He wrote an e-mail to his father in which Grant finally confronted him. Told him what he felt and how much he missed him. His father replied weeks later. He told his son where he was, but never spoke about what his son had written. At least it was a start, a chance for Grant to understand he had a right to speak and a right to be loved.

Meanwhile, Trish and I worked together on ways to teach both Grant and Connor to act more responsibly. That included treating her with respect. Christmas was the moment of truth. She had managed to work extra shifts and bought the iPods. But the preparations for Christmas were exhausting her. She wanted a tree, the house cleaned, baking done. She wanted to give the boys perfect presents. The boys had been refusing to help. Even when she pulled the artificial tree out of her basement, they refused to set it up, much less do any of the decorating. The next time we met, she was angry. "I deserve better," she said. I agreed. We decided she would protest by not setting up the tree. Either her sons would make a contribution to the family Christmas, or Christmas was not going to be what they expected.

That was our last meeting before the holidays. I admit to thinking about Trish on Christmas morning when, at my in-laws', I sat opening gifts that had been placed beneath a tree with ornaments collected for generations. When I met Trish and the boys after the holidays, both Grant and Connor had their iPods in their laps.

"We didn't have a tree," Trish told me. The boys avoided my eyes.

"How was that for you both?" I asked, not letting the boys get off the hook easily.

To my delight, Grant answered first. "I missed the tree," he said, and looked at his mother.

"We spoke about it after," Connor said. "Mom was right. We should've helped some."

We didn't need to speak much more about what had gone wrong. Trish had done what she needed to do to teach her boys about compassion for others. They had their iPods. They knew very well how hard she'd worked to make that happen. They also felt awful about not having done what she had asked them to do. Those lessons were learned. No further lecture was needed.

Besides, there were successes to celebrate. The boys had used their birthday money to buy Trish a lovely set of earrings that she was wearing and showed me. And they'd done the dishes after Christmas dinner.

In the following weeks, things improved further. Trish met a new partner, and the boys seemed to like him. "He's real good with computers," Connor told me. There were other small changes, too. Trish had gotten fed up with the boys' eating all the good food the day after she bought it, gobbling down all the soda pop and chips and leaving nothing for her Saturday night video-fest. With some coaching, she agreed it was time the boys started to take responsibility for the groceries. Once a week, she takes one of them with her shopping. Most weeks, Grant volunteers, which is fine by Connor, who would rather be with his girlfriend than with his mother. Grant is given twenty-five dollars for junk food. It's up to him to buy whatever he can, but it has to last all week.

Since she'd started doing that, the food lasts longer and Grant is careful to portion it out. He also doesn't mind buying the budget cola and no-name chips. "You get twice as much that way," he told me. He is also showing a lot more care for others' feelings. The last time I spoke to him about shopping, it was Connor who volunteered that Grant had bought him a special frozen treat that the family can't normally afford. "I know how much Connor likes those things," Grant said, smiling.

Being There

Grant and Connor might not be perfect, but Trish is doing much to help them develop more responsibility, despite the hard knocks they've suffered from their father. They've taught me that our children can heal. It is never too late to be there for them. Thinking about what Trish did, we see that children learn compassion and responsibility when they are shown how to love and respect others. Success is more likely when parents apply the following principles:

- *Avoid anger:* If Trish had met Grant's anger with more anger, Grant would probably have escalated his behavior further. He still wouldn't have felt heard. He would have learned that anger is the only acceptable response when you are feeling hurt. His repertoire of emotions would have remained narrow. Better to show children other emotions. When we cry, we give them permission to cry, too.

- *Don't give up:* Persistence pays. It might have been easy for Trish to give up. To abandon her sons in the same way that Clarence had. To stop believing in them. Instead, she set boundaries. She understood that her job of teaching them was far from over. I may have helped keep her motivated and smoothed over the rough edges of the family's communication, but it was Trish's spirit and her desire to make her life and her sons' lives better that helped the family find healthier ways to relate to one another.

- *Model appropriate behavior:* One of the interventions I used midway through our time together was to ask Grant about the different rules at his father's and mother's homes. At his father's house, it was pretty obvious what the overarching rule governing people's behavior was: Do things that are good for yourself. Do things that make you feel in control, like giving Grant's room to the baby. Ignore what anyone else wants, even if it means giving away the family pet. Mom had a different house rule: Do things that are good for others. Work an extra shift to pay for Christmas presents. Stand by your kid, no matter what. Love unconditionally. It was easier to help Grant and Connor behave more responsibly with Trish modeling for them We-thinking behavior.

- *Hold others accountable:* When mistakes are made, it's not the end of the world. It's an opportunity to teach our children the consequences of their actions. Trish knew this from growing up in a family where she was expected to look after her six younger brothers and sisters and where not being pushed to complete her education had meant she ended up with few career options. Trish understood cause and effect. She was happy to find gentle ways to teach her children the same: If they are eating all the snack food and not thinking enough about sharing, then put them in charge of buying it. Sometimes, straightforward actions speak louder than endless lectures.

- *Help children to name their feelings:* We aren't by nature very good at piecing together what we feel. The more we can help our kids to understand what they are feeling and to describe those feelings, the stronger they will be during emotional crises. That means we adults need to give kids an emotional vocabulary. Grant wasn't just angry. Trish and I helped him realize he was also hurt, sad, and feeling abandoned. Those are more complex emotions to decipher, but ones he'll need to understand if he is to figure out his relationship with his father. They're also emotions he'll need later, if and when he finds himself in an intimate adult relationship. Without those names for feelings, he runs the risk of becoming just as emotionally abusive to his partner as Clarence was to Trish.

The Advantage of Being Close

Of course, Trish has one advantage above all others. She is physically there. Listening to Grant and Connor speak, I sensed their great longing to have their father back. An e-mail dad was just not going to cut it. Any advantage that our virtual connections give us is only realized if we back them up with connections more intimate.

At the end of the day, touch trumps text.

Not that a virtual hug can't warm our hearts if the message is intimate enough. It's just that it's not enough without the flesh, blood, and scent of others to anchor our memories to the tactile roots of experience.

If we really want children like Grant and Connor to think globally and experience the advantages that a connected world has to offer, we are going to have to guarantee them very genuine connections with ourselves first. That means parents, schools, and communities are going to have show compassion for our youth and raise them with a sense of responsibility for themselves and others. This We Generation is not unlike the Me Generation before them. The difference is that where the Me Generation struggled to "Think globally, act locally," this next graduating class, if held in the embrace of families and communities that give a damn, will have unrestricted access to a global community in which to share themselves. The members of this generation will be able to think and act globally as effortlessly as they can think and act locally.

Tips List

There are lots of ways parents can model compassion for their children. Here are a few tips from parents who are doing just that.

- Put money in a street musician's hat. Doing so, a parent models that when we appreciate people making our community more fun, we show that appreciation.
- Say hello to a panhandler. Look him in the eye, and acknowledge him as a person. One needn't give money to him directly. Instead, make an annual contribution to an organization that helps people who spend their days on the streets.

- Model how to share your time with others, even when it's not convenient.
- Feed people less fortunate than you.
- Do something for others that doesn't involve your workplace. Your children will understand this to be a less self-serving way of giving to others.
- Watch the news together with your children, if doing so is age-appropriate, and then discuss what you see. Try watching news with an international perspective to help your children think about global issues from different points of view.
- Be charitable more than once a year.
- Make a daily offering.
- Tithe, contribute to a charity regularly, or donate a small amount of money to a child's preferred cause.
- If you have people working for you, share your staff (like a cleaning lady's time or a secretary's skills) with another person when he or she is in need.
- Be a host family for someone from another country or culture.
- Talk about social justice issues.
- If you or your child is treated unfairly, involve the child in the process of organizing for his or her rights.

chapter **four**

Please Touch

When Richard was born, his mother, Tammy, told the social workers who looked in on her that she could manage. The social workers had lots of reasons to be concerned. Tammy had been removed from her mother at birth and was raised in a number of foster homes. She never made it past grade three academically. She'd spent her entire life in the care of the state. She'd been institutionalized on more than one occasion with severe depression. She carried a string of diagnoses. It all added up to a mother with little capacity to care for her child.

In hindsight, maybe Richard should have been taken into care. But Tammy followed through on all her commitments to her son. She got him to doctor's appointments when he needed them. Her home was kept tidy, and there were always enough toys and baby formula. She was friendly with the public health nurse who visited. When Richard was a bit older and could be left in day-care, Tammy trained as a cook's assistant. She always made sure she picked up Richard at the right time and that he came to day-care with a clean set of extra clothes.

For a time, it looked as if Richard was going to do all right.

It wasn't until he was nearing age three that the child-care professionals working with Richard noticed how withdrawn he was. He always seemed like an outcast in any playgroup. It was as if he didn't know how to play with other children. One of Richard's caregivers used to joke, "He's like a puppy that's not been socialized right. He doesn't know what to do with the other kids."

It didn't help that Richard's intelligence appeared to be at about the same level as his mother's. No one expected much from a boy who didn't know his colors, couldn't count to twenty, and spoke with a thick country accent people in the city laughed at. When other children could speak in full sentences, Richard mumbled simple things like, "I want cookie."

By the time Richard was in first grade, he was already behind. He was held back a year, but it didn't help. Not being promoted just made him feel more self-conscious. He became a loner. He was polite to the special-education teacher, but never seemed to do any of his homework. Tammy couldn't understand what the fuss was about. "He don't cause you no trouble, does he?" she kept asking his teachers. To her, Richard was a well-behaved little boy doing just fine.

The story gets worse. By seventh grade, Richard was an awkward boy with crooked teeth that ached from never being brushed. He came to school dressed in secondhand clothes and was teased because of it. He was pasty white and slight of build. He quickly became a target for bullies, who sensed he was easy prey. He only complained once, when three boys kidnapped him and tied him up naked in the park. When the police brought him home, Tammy asked him where his clothes were. She said she didn't have time to be buying him new clothes every time he got into a tussle at school.

The bullying subsided after that, but Richard was too afraid to go to school most days. When he finally did get to class, he did little or no work. The school offered him lots of help. It even arranged with a local orthodontist to fix his teeth. First, though, he would need a dentist to fill the twelve cavities he had. His diet of colas, potato chips, and frozen dinners had taken their toll. His body was a mess.

None of the help offered came to much. Richard became more and more isolated during junior high. He stopped going to the dentist. He stayed in his room and played computer games on an old machine a church group had donated to the family for Christmas. After a time, most people forgot about Richard.

Looking back, we can see that although Richard wasn't deprived of the basics of life, he was deprived of compassion. His mother looked after him as best she could, but she had no capacity to make him do what children are apt to not want to do, like brush their teeth, eat vegetables, do their homework, or read. A compassionate parent forces a child to do these things. A neglectful one does not.

Worst of all, Richard's mother seldom touched her son. From an early age, she handled him only when it was necessary. Richard grew up without gentle caresses. He seldom knew an embrace. He was rarely asked what he wanted or how his day went at school. Psychologically, emotionally, spiritually, Richard grew up untouched and disconnected.

He had never been shown how to live outside his home. He had never taken a bus or been to the mall. He'd never been on a sleepover. He'd also never been told who his father was. Richard was living in an emotional vacuum. Psychologically, he was still breathing, but just barely.

We Need to Touch

Compassion is conveyed through touch. It needn't be physical, though it worries me when I meet a child like Richard who has known practically no loving physical contact with anyone. If we want our children to think more We than Me, we are going to have to show them through our actions, as much as through our words, how important they are to us.

Admittedly, few children are as isolated as Richard. However, in our anxiety to protect our children, I am worried we have overcompensated for a time when children's bodies were violated too often by those they were supposed to trust. We mustn't forget that through touch, physical and emotional, we grow. The compassion of another is conveyed through his gaze. A look of admiration and a hearty pat on the back can chase away self-doubt. Both can lift a child's spirit.

Holy Roman Emperor Frederick II (1194–1250) is reported to have raised several children in isolation to see which language they would speak when of an age to talk. There was no doubt in the emperor's mind that children have an innate language. Today we know better. Children learn language, and just about everything else, through interaction with others. Historian Adrianna Benzaquén tells us that all the children died during those early experiments. According to her research, chronicles from the time reported that the children "could not live without clappings of the hands, and gestures, and gladness of countenance, and blandishments."[1]

Eight hundred years later, a thirteen-year-old girl known in the press as Genie (her real name was Susan Wiley) made headlines in November 1970, when she was discovered to have been a virtual prisoner in her parents' home, completely neglected her entire life. Her parents were arrested, and Genie was placed into the treatment and care of the Childrens Hospital in Los Angeles. In this case, what Benzaquén calls a "forbidden experiment" had taken place, giving developmental scientists the chance to understand what happens when children are deprived of nurturing. What the researchers learned was that maturation doesn't just occur naturally: "Although the girl was thirteen years old, she was unable to talk or walk, wore diapers, and did not know the most basic life skills (like chewing). Her limbs and muscles were partially atrophied owing to physical restraint and inadequate activity."[2]

Richard has not suffered such harsh neglect, and most children are touched enough to ensure normal development. But are they touched enough to learn the foundations of compassion? Or of responsibility? Or of citizenship?

The Many Disguises of Touch

I've learned that touch comes in many disguises. It's a cultural thing.

Shortly after being elected in 2006, Prime Minister Stephen Harper of Canada was caught on camera dropping his ten-year-old son, Ben, off at school. With a stiff, fatherly handshake, he said good-bye while his secret service escort stood warily watching. That handshake made the evening news. Harper was subjected to a barrage of criticism. "He should have hugged his son," I heard one man complain. "What an awful role model for fathers," said another.

I thought, Who are we to judge? Not all ten-year-olds want hugs from their fathers captured on national television.

To be truthful, putting politics aside, what impressed me more was that Harper had seen his son off to school at all. How many dads, let alone leaders of nations, take the time to connect with their children each morning? Some dads do, but millions of others don't. Sometimes, the best a dad or mom can manage is to shout last-minute instructions as the kids charge out the back door.

I was impressed that Harper had made the effort to drop his son off at school. He was there with him during a time of great change for his son. I imagine that Harper would have given his boy a hug if the situation had been different. A month earlier, he'd been photographed joyfully embracing his entire family on the stage of the election hall when his election win was announced.

Maybe we were quick to criticize Harper because we are afraid our own children aren't getting the hugs they need, from us. Afraid that if we avoid hugs, our children will look to others for the intimacy they are missing, and that the others may be less trustworthy.

Who might our children look to? Sexual partners are a poor substitute for teenagers looking for intimacy from parents. Touch is confused with sex, love with intercourse.

And then there are those who give up looking, who swallow their need for contact along with a dose of legal and illegal substances that help them ignore the pain of abandonment. Or those who distract themselves with mind-numbing marathons of video gaming and "reality" TV. The only clue to their isolation is their surliness.

The unconnected child snarls at authority. In contrast, the connected child who experiences intimacy is self-conscious about the effect his actions have on others. He thinks before he blurts something offensive. Determining which path a child follows most often falls to those who raise him: his parents and other important caregivers.

Touched by Family

A family is . . . well, just about any group of people who care for one another's welfare. Add children to the mix, and the number of things families are expected to do grows exponentially. Little ones need nurturing, and feeding, and to be taught what they need to know. It's astounding that most families measure up quite well. That, despite the statistic that on average, according to one survey, children aged thirteen and fourteen spend just thirty-eight minutes a day with their fathers and just twenty-one minutes a day with their mothers in direct child-centered activities, such as being transported to activities, eating together, or being helped with homework.[3] Preschoolers fare better, of course: Mothers spend about two and a half hours a day in care activities, and fathers average ninety minutes. All in all, it's not much.

Our kids adapt. The sometimes idealized era of the postwar bungalow with the stay-at-home mom and the breadwinning dad has passed. Though many women and men of the twenty-first century would like a better career-life balance, restricting one parent or the other to a particular role is not the way to achieve it. Besides, it's unlikely we'll be looking backward anytime soon. Of every ten students in college, six are women. That number holds across almost all disciplines, from medicine to theater arts, environmental science to psychology. Traditionally, men's earnings outpaced women's, while women typically provided management of the home and taught their children compassion through their presence. That stereotype is shifting, like beach sand after a tidal surge. Men aren't going to be earning more than their much-better-educated wives for long and aren't going to be left out of the child-rearing, either. The right to choose is growing. Our lives are being parsed into emotionally fulfilling morsels. We can work and parent with some supports.

Nonetheless, someone has to clean toilets, stock diaper drawers, and make pot roast, at least when the children are young. We need creative ways to help parents live fulfilling lives while still being there to embrace their kids.

I prefer to imagine what can be rather than remain stuck in a revisionist past. The 1950s weren't as great as we think they were. Spousal abuse was far more prevalent than today. Children were frequent witnesses to violence. There was a higher incidence of child abuse. Sexual abuse of children, at home and in our institutions, went practically unchallenged. There were few, if any, kids' help lines, school-based abuse prevention programs, or services for runaways. Children who were touched badly or witnesses to brutality at home were left to grow up and repeat the cycle of one bad touch after another.

I prefer what we have today. I prefer this world, where family sovereignty is not absolute and children can be helped when help is needed.

What Touch Means to a Child

Looked at this way, we are in an enviable position to encourage our children to be touched. I'm not talking reckless abandonment—quite the contrary. I've worked with too many children like Richard whose stories of abuse make my stomach clench. But after we have done the police checks, instituted the no-touch policies, doubled the bathroom monitors, ensured that our children are never vulnerable to the predators we are sure are lurking, what then? Will we allow our children a positive embrace? A warm and thoughtful hug from a teacher or coach when they need encouragement and support?

Child psychologist Anna Freud, daughter of Sigmund Freud, is among the most authoritative voices on the subject of children's attachments. Working with children after the Second World War, she reported that those who were sent away to foster homes outside London to avoid the blitz were more traumatized than those who stayed with their parents and experienced the bombing. It's a lesson we should heed. Children are far more resilient to dramatic upheaval when there is someone they trust holding them close.

Of course, how families share such intimacy varies across cultures and communities. While some aspects of attachment look the same the world over (rocking a child in one's arms, cooing, and singing to her), parents show their love in many ways that are very specific to their own culture. For example, as psychologist Shi Lin explains in her look at Asian American families and the stereotypes surrounding their parenting styles, a parent who appears from another culture's perspective to be aloof in her relationship with her children may not see herself that way at all.[4] Nor do her children experience her as distant or cold; instead, they recognize their parent's respect for their personal integrity.

When the actions of people in a particular culture are judged by the standards of cultural outsiders, there is the risk of misunderstanding. Even within cultures, people have different styles. I make few assumptions these days about the right way to convey to a child love and connection. Instead, I am inclined to ask children if they feel loved and to wait for an answer.

Touch Zones

Even the unruly child needs connections, not punishment. Perry Good has written a great deal about getting kids to act responsibly at school.[5] Her goal has been to create respectful educational environments in which our children behave as we'd like them to behave. Though we may blame the kids for their smart-ass attitudes these days, Good thinks a culture of disrespect is rooted in how kids are treated beyond their classrooms. It's said the apple doesn't fall far from the tree. Our children learn what we teach them.

I have to wonder how compassionate no-touch policies are when they infiltrate our schools. When she was a new graduate with her master's degree in education, Good found herself in the Lower East Side of Manhattan at Public School 71 in front of a class of eighth-graders who had exhausted and chased away a healthy number of teachers before her:

> In spite of the fact that the school had some dangerous qualities, I liked the kids. They were, underneath it all, just regular eighth-graders—sassy, adorable, out of control, and caring. They acted like four-year-olds one minute, and twenty-two-year-olds the next. As I began to know them better, I asked them about teacher #10. The students said they had emptied the contents of her purse into a metal trash can in the classroom, set it on fire, and then thrown in the purse. She left screaming. I asked them why they did it. They looked around the classroom at each other, and I could tell they were wondering whether or not to share this information with me. Finally, one of the girls, Elsie, quietly said, "She wouldn't touch us." Those words still echo in my head after all these years. What these kids wanted, like

all kids want, was to simply have their teacher treat them like human beings, to touch them, to care about them, to connect with them.[6]

Treating our children like this creates what Good calls the "background tapestry" for learning. I would say it teaches our children how to think about others. It brings them a little closer to cementing their connections with those who can make them feel as if they matter.

Advocating more good touch is not at all the same as suggesting we neglect our responsibility to protect our children from bad touch. It's an awful, unfortunate truth that babysitters, priests, coaches, teachers, and, yes, parents, too, sometimes abuse their access to children. There have been too many victims for us not to feel anxious. It is estimated that as many as 80 percent of female adult prisoners were sexually abused as children, and as many as one-third of male offenders were abused. Compassionate touch encourages our capacity to connect; abusive touch corrupts it.

The good news is that the frequency of physical interference and bad touching is decreasing. According to the U.S. Department of Justice, of the more than 200,000 abductions of children committed in the United States each year, as few as 100 are by complete strangers, and this number has decreased by more than half since the late 1980s.[7] While even one abduction is too many, the incidence of abductions, sexual assault, and physical abuse is remaining stable or dropping.[8] This, despite the increased reporting today because children now are more likely to disclose abuse when they experience it.[9] A great deal of effort across North America to prevent abuse has been paying off, though television newscasts would make us think otherwise. It takes only one child like Madeleine McCann, the abducted three-year-old taken from her hotel room in southern Portugal in May 2007, to send a collective shiver down every parent's spine. What we forget amid the panic is that our efforts to make children safe have been quite successful. Coaches receive many days of training on how to touch children properly; abuse by clergy is now disclosed and the problem is dealt with rather than moved to another community; children are taught about good touch and bad touch in school; and the police are improving their capacity to catch pedophiles on the Internet.

So what harm do we do, now that precautions are in place, when we deny our children the (nonsexual) intimacy of an adult's attention? That attention may take many forms: one-on-one time, a hearty embrace, a respectful gift, or a heart-to-heart talk. What damage do we risk if we raise children in the vacuum of no-touch policies and zero-tolerance worlds that leave kids without role models of how to touch and be touched?

Those are the children I worry about.

I saw the value of touch firsthand at a school high in a hillside slum called Público, in Medellín, Colombia. It is not a safe place in which to travel, much less raise a family. This was formerly the home of Pablo Escobar, the drug lord who for years dominated the Colombian drug trade with the United States. Among the dirt roads and tin-roofed houses of Público can be found criminal gangs, Colombian military, municipal police, and paramilitary soldiers, all equally well armed. It's difficult to know whom to trust. The local militias who appoint themselves to protect people from the drug gangs are known to be as cruel as any of the other armed forces and pose significant danger to noncombatants.

The children of Público know the sound of gunfire. In at least one incident, children have been killed by stray bullets aimed at others outside the boundary of their schoolyard fence.

I met Vilma Salazar in that school. She is the voice of compassion and education for a thousand children between the ages of five and eighteen. The children attend in two shifts. The classrooms are stacked three floors high, those on the ground floor opening onto verandahs that form cement walkways in front of shutterless windows. One can be forgiven for not noticing the condition of the immediate grounds, because the view out over the volcanic valley is stunning. Above the city's haze, you can see green hills and rolling mountain peaks. The houses step down into the valley, like a staircase. Cars zigzag their way up the winding roads, as brightly colored buses adorned with hand-painted crafts spew black exhaust and bully drivers to yield.

Vilma knows every child at the school by name. As she proudly shows me around, children swarm behind us. They pack together in gray-uniformed clumps. They stare at me, point, and then giggle. As we move, so they follow.

I'm there for my research. That work is seeking to understand why some children survive and thrive despite exposure to great adversity such as violence, poverty, migration, war, sexual exploitation, abuse, and neglect. Not all children go down the dangerous paths that we might expect them to follow after such experiences.

Watching Vilma, I am given a clue. Each child who comes up to her is greeted by name. Then she embraces each with a big hug and plants upon their cheeks a kiss. It is the kind of kiss that comes with two hands cupping a child's face so that eyes meet. In that moment, this short little woman tells that child, "You are important to me," without needing to say a word.

I can tell she loves these children. What's more, she respects them. They have all shown courage. They have made their way through dangerous streets to get to school. Vilma tells me that their parents counsel them that if they hear gunfire, they must find shelter behind brick walls—crouch, wait—but then continue on to school.

I'm embarrassed when I hear such stories. I laugh at how silly my worry for my own children seems in this context. I remember telling my daughter when she was nine to listen to the crossing guard and my eleven-year old son not to linger too late on the school grounds after school.

Seeing Vilma with these children, I understand why they come to school. This is a place where they feel wanted. This is a place of calm and hope. This is a place where they remain sheltered from risk. It's their lifeline.

Even the ungainly fourteen-year-old whom Vilma catches throwing the janitor's broom over the cliff, and who gets a stern finger-wagging for it, understands how much he is valued here. Vilma makes the boy climb through a hole in the fence at the edge of the playground and bring back the broom. After placing it by the janitor's shed, he lumbers over to her. Like an ungainly adolescent giraffe, all towering angularity, he cranes his face down awkwardly toward her, finding a place to rest his head on his principal's shoulder. She cradles the small of his back with one arm and, like a mother, cups his pubescent cheek with her free hand. Then she places a light kiss on his cheek. Forgiveness given, she thumps him on the shoulders, a rough shake that says how much she appreciates his obedience. He straightens and we walk on, her job with this one complete. At least for now. I turn and see the boy join his friends, who poke him in the ribs, teasing. Perhaps, I think, they are jostling him out of envy. Or shame, knowing how much they too seek such an embrace.

Lessons Learned

I can't help but think there is much we can learn from Vilma. When was the last time the principal at your child's school gave your child a hug for a job well done, a high five, or a pat on the back? We have polluted our minds with the threat of child abuse. Our overprotectiveness may be denying our children the very connections that would prevent them from becoming the mouthy disrespectful teenagers we abhor. If we are to wrestle our children from violence, apathy, and shame, we would do well to imitate that diminutive woman teaching on the hillsides of Medellín. She does some profoundly important things that we parents should take to heart:

- She models for the children the appropriate way to touch and be touched.
- She shows how to forgive mistakes.
- She holds children accountable, expecting them to make things right when things go wrong.
- She is consistent—is there every day for the kids.
- She knows the children by name, recognizing their uniqueness.
- She offers them a safe place to grow.
- She offers them a sense of community within the walls of the school.
- She offers them a place to make a contribution.

Do our schools do so well? Do our families, neighborhoods, and communities offer children these same roots?

Learning About Touch in Positive Ways

We run the risk of missing the chance to help our children learn about compassion through touch when we overcontrol them. Sadly, we no longer seem to let them

- push or shove anyone;
- throw snowballs;
- wrestle;
- play rough;
- share lip gloss, makeup, or be seen to be applying anything on anyone;
- point anything at anyone, not a banana or a stick;
- hug or let themselves be hugged, unless by their parents.

And the list goes on.

If we remove all touch from our children's lives, how will they ever understand the difference between good touch and bad touch? If we never let them throw a snowball, how will they understand the difference between a snowball packed too hard and a snowball that explodes when it lands on another child's shoulder? While I want no child to be hurt as a consequence of the recklessness of another, our children need to figure some of this out themselves.

It's too easy to blame children for their selfishness and lack of connections when the fault must be shared. We can do more. But that doesn't mean doting on our children and making them our pets. Only a few days after I met Vilma, I was back in North America at an airport waiting for my next flight. As chance would have it, I met a couple I know, two physicians, who were enthralled with their first child, a robust four-month-old with the chubby cheeks that come from breast-feeding and a sweet smell of baby powder beneath his trendy Gap sleeper. His parents watched his every twitch. Their faces beamed. They proudly told me he was potty trained. I was a little confused when they told me this. I thought I must have misheard them, the jet lag and all.

"He signals us. With his finger." The boy's mother made a small gesture with her index finger, as if she was tapping out music. "That tells us he has to go potty. You can train children to do that," she says proudly. "You just have to be really connected to your child. Like in Africa. Children there don't wear diapers. The mothers just know when the child needs to go."

I check my watch to see when my flight needs to go. I'm hesitant to say much. It all feels a little creepy. At least, I note, staring down at the infant asleep in his stroller, there is still the big bottom bulge of a diaper on the baby. Obviously, the child isn't so well trained as to be trusted on an airplane.

I nod politely, but I'm thinking, This is not connection. This is a circus trick. If an African mother, whom I have seen, knows when to take her child from the swaddling cloth on her back and gingerly hold the child away from her so that the child can relieve himself, it is because that mother senses her baby on her back. The child's hot skin is just a layer of fabric away. There is the child's anxious squirm. His bowels are hers, the symbiosis of connection precontemplative. There is no trick or training, just physical bonding.

I look at the four-month-old in front of me, and worry. What happens when he is fourteen and decides that getting As are not his thing? That he doesn't want every part of his life to be an expression of what his parents can achieve? What if he just wants to be a kid? Without the pressure to be out ahead of everyone else? Will he be able to break free of these oppressive expectations? Will he find the unconditional acceptance that is the root of compassion?

The child snuggling on his mother's back is connected in a way that this four-month-old in his stroller at the airport is not. Frankly, we would do better to swaddle his bottom and pick him up, sheltering him, close against us, rather than leaving him so very alone and apart.

This is not connection. This is the illusion of togetherness.

This is not going to produce a healthy child. When we engage more physically with our kids, we not only tamper with their tempers, smooth their moods, and help them understand their connections to others, but also affect their brain development. The better-attached child suffers fewer neurological disorders. Children who are touched suffer less from the symptoms of trauma, depression, anxiety, regulatory and sleep disorders, pervasive developmental disorders, and just plain being miserable. Maybe that's why even rats lick their young. Denied this contact, a baby rat doesn't function well as an adult. In humans, a lack of touch can make a child feel isolated and the world seem an inhospitable and distant place. Frigid and cold, children denied touch offer no resistance when others demand obedience of them. They expect no one to be sensitive to their needs.

Being There

I was hospitalized for a week when I was five years old. That time away from my parents was my first and, I think my most vivid, early memory. It wasn't supposed to be traumatic, but it was. My fear grew from the very first night, when I woke up feeling very uncomfortable. My parents had gone home. They weren't allowed to stay all night. I was strapped to the bed in traction and couldn't get up to go to the bathroom. I remember trying to call someone, but none of the nurses came quickly enough. To this day, I feel embarrassed thinking about that moment, crying like a baby, wetting myself. It was such a long time before anyone came.

Such reflections have made me sensitive to the needs of children in my work. What they experience is often not what we adults intend. Words like *wait* and *soon* mean little to a child who needs comfort.

I don't know if we ever really grow out of our neediness. Nor do I think we should. We are healthier for being joined to our families and communities. We live longer when we have friends. People in committed relationships generally report a better sense of well-being and are more satisfied sexually.[10]

The traditional Chinese character for love includes the symbols for the heart and friendship in balance: the passion of fused hearts joined with the intimacy that comes from an emotional bond with a friend. We can learn from that. Touch without emotional intimacy does not instill compassion. Emotional intimacy without touch leaves us feeling less than complete.

It is estimated that 30 to 45 percent of children are insecurely attached, meaning they're not confident that someone will be there to meet their needs.[11] They are not touched enough (or, depending on the culture, spoken to and cooed at) to gain a sense of attachment, nor are the emotional bonds with their caregivers sufficiently tensile to honor the child's need for both security and freedom.

If she waits too long to get a response to a hungry cry or a bruised knee, a child might experience a "tear in their relationship," as Linda Wark explains in *Family Therapy*

Magazine.[12] Children will do anything they can to sew that tear back up, even if it means hiding from their emotions or withdrawing from those whom they depend on for consistent support.

Unfortunately, parents sometimes reach out to their children in the most inappropriate of ways. Instead of the attention (and touch) that children really want from us, they are offered harmful substitutes:

- We buy them lots of expensive toys that they play with by themselves, when what they really want is our attention.
- We are too permissive, when what they really want is boundaries and the security of knowing that someone cares enough to enforce these limits.
- We overprotect them when they need to experience risk and adventure.
- We touch them to satisfy our needs for warmth and connection, ignoring their need to move toward intimate relationships with others.

None of these strategies will help our children grow into card-carrying members of a We Generation. It's more likely they will drift from our homes into relationships where they can be manipulated, recreating exactly what they've already experienced at home: a lack of genuine compassion for what they need.

Connected but Still Neglected

Taken to an extreme, depriving a child of touch inflicts damage to her psyche. Ten-year-old Rhonda shows all the signs of that kind of damage. Though extreme, her life story has something valuable to teach us about the healing that comes with touch.

For a long time now, Rhonda has had no one to touch her except the professionals who come and go as her caseworkers. Their presence is an anthology of short stories to a girl who needs a full-length novel. There are few who know her full history. Rhonda survives the changes by being as bad as she can be. At least that way, the professionals keep coming.

When Rhonda was just eleven months old, she was removed from her mother, who was putting alcohol in her bottle to quiet her hungry screams. Sometimes, when she kept crying, her mother burned her with cigarettes or left her for hours alone in her crib, soiled and scabbed from the neglect. Eventually, Rhonda was placed with the aunt who had reported her sister's neglect to the authorities. With five other children already living in her aunt's home, Rhonda quickly became invisible amid the mayhem. She was fed and cleaned, but no one paid her much attention otherwise. Rhonda's new family thought most about hard work. They owned a tree farm and a portable mill. The kids were expected to earn their keep and given a "kick in the arse" if they didn't contribute by doing their chores. When Rhonda began to act out in school, mouthing off at her teachers or fighting on the playground, her aunt and uncle just shrugged. They figured she would leave school soon enough, anyway. There was work to be done at home. It mattered little whether Rhonda got an education or not.

Rhonda's mother disappeared to the streets. She turned up dead of a drug overdose when Rhonda was seven. It was hard to tell, her aunt said, whether Rhonda ever understood why her mother had died, much less why she'd abandoned her.

By grade four, Rhonda had become known as a determined girl who refused to attend French classes and was disruptive in most others. Her behavior kept getting her referred for extra help. She seemed to like the attention of the one-on-one workers who would sit close by her in class and help her with her studies. But her motivation to please seldom lasted very long. When her behavior became too unsettled, she was suspended. She didn't mind. She'd march out of the school shouting, "I got a suspension! I don't have to come to school!" She seemed to like being known as a problem kid.

When she got home, her aunt would shake her head and then turn back to her office, which was above a warehouse the family had built on their property. Rhonda was expected to stay out of the way, to be neither seen nor heard. Her aunt made it clear to the school that she had no time to supervise Rhonda or to make sure that her niece did the homework they sent home with her.

Not surprisingly, at home, Rhonda obeyed the rules. She was quiet, did as she was told, avoided conflict. At school, she was only a terror when she was in class. Oddly, when she was on the playground among peers who didn't know her as well as her classmates did, she could be caring and helpful. But in class, under the gaze of her teacher, Rhonda seemed to provoke anger from anyone who tried to reach out to her.

Rhonda was offered counseling, but it really wasn't what she needed. A counselor is just not enough for a child like Rhonda. She needed a close connection with someone whom she could see every day and who would offer her compassion, touch, and reasonable expectations: someone who wouldn't harm her, who would understand that her anger was justified, and who would be there for her when she cooled down after an eruption. I thought of Vilma in Colombia and realized that Rhonda needed far more than the material well-being and education we were offering her.

There were clues, though, that Rhonda might be ready to be touched and might be willing to reciprocate. The first sign was Rhonda's willingness to make a contribution at her aunt's. To their credit, her adopted family had for years made it clear that Rhonda had responsibilities. Though they'd shown her little compassion, at least they'd taught her that her actions mattered. If her chores weren't done right, and on time, she heard about it. The second clue that Rhonda wanted connections was found at school, where she sought the attention of her peers and teachers. Though she seemed most comfortable garnering negative attention, at least we knew she still wanted others to notice her.

With the right attachments, I was confident Rhonda could change. I am as idealistic in this regard as A. S. Neill was half a century ago, when he wrote about Summerhill, a radical experiment in educating children with respect and in an atmosphere of participatory democracy. The school he founded in Britain encouraged displays of compassion and accountability. There, children were encouraged to be genuinely themselves while still being an active part of the community created around them. As Neill said: "Hate breeds hate, love breeds love."[13] It was love that he was seeking to cultivate.

My attention quickly turned from Rhonda to her school and its potential to convey love to a child who was growing up without the love of a parent. At least there, it seemed, Rhonda might experience a compassionate connection with someone special. Fortunately, the school was willing to help. Our strategy might seem naive, but it worked.

First, we carefully chose one teacher's aide who would work with Rhonda and really get to know the girl. The teacher's aide was an older woman who had raised her own children. Best of all, she was not about to change jobs. She could commit to Rhonda for at least two years. Rhonda would no longer receive out-of-school suspensions. Discipline, when necessary, would only mean more time with her teacher's aide.

Second, Rhonda was given responsibility for others at school. She was expected to act as responsibly toward children in younger grades as she did at home. She took on the roles of monitor and reading coach for five-year-olds. Part of the educational plan for her was to teach her about child development. She was shown how to care for small children, all the while being cared for herself.

Being shown compassion helped Rhonda increase her capacity to show compassion toward others, and then to herself. She was expected to act responsibly, and she did. The more she felt that she belonged, and was held in an emotional embrace by her school and its staff, the better her behavior became. Now when she was suspended, she was expected to take on more responsibilities around her school, not fewer. Her attachment to her teacher's aide never wavered.

It wasn't a perfect cure, but it was a start. Eventually, the teacher's aide was coached on how to talk with Rhonda about the loss of her mother. Slowly, Rhonda began to speak, first with the aide, then in a counselor's office with the aide joining in for support. Mostly, Rhonda wanted to know the facts. What happened to her as a baby? Was her mother really dead? Did other children like her feel the same?

Rhonda was lucky enough to have a school that cared and the supports she needed. She eventually healed. Unfortunately, there are many other children who are provided with far less. Excluded, teased, and isolated, they can become depressed or angry—often both. That's how it was for Eric Harris and Dylan Klebold, the two young men who killed twelve of their classmates and a teacher and wounded twenty-three others before killing themselves at Columbine High School in Littleton, Colorado, on April 20, 1999. Not long before the attack, Klebold wrote: "As I look for love I feel I can't find it, ever."

Five Steps to Connecting During a Crisis

We can only spoil a child when we lack compassion for him or her. If we are thinking about our children's needs from their point of view, there is little chance of harm.

Take time-outs, for example. They're not unlike school suspensions. Let's not fool ourselves. Time-outs are for us parents to calm down, collect our thoughts, have a cup of coffee, and center ourselves on the task of loving our recalcitrant child—the one up in his room kicking the door and screaming, "I hate you! I hate you! You're a poopy face! I hate you!" (or something like that).

A well-socialized child needs to quickly move from banishment to reconnection, which means parents being ready and willing to calm down and forgive. Our children need us to help them make amends. The time-out, or suspension, should be only the first of a five-step process—calm, reflect, reconnect, fix, and embrace—that helps children understand their connections to others and models for them what compassion looks like in action. Consider what you might do if your jealous five-year-old daughter mangles her little brother's new action figure that he just received for his birthday:

1. *Calm:* Both you and your daughter need to calm down and temporarily separate. Placing a child in her own space, like a bedroom, for a few minutes conveys to the child the message that being with other people requires better, more thoughtful behavior. Removing yourself, too, to a quiet space, is a good idea so you can gather your thoughts and think carefully about what to do next. If the child is a little older (and other children are looked after), there is nothing wrong with taking a few minutes to walk the block in front of your house while you think.

2. *Reflect:* Your daughter needs to reflect on what she did and how her actions have affected others. That means asking her to review what just happened and explaining how her behavior made other people feel. A younger child needs concrete examples: "You made your brother sad when you broke his toy. He was crying and his eyes are all red. I'll have to get him a new toy, and that doesn't make me very happy."

3. *Reconnect:* Your daughter needs opportunities to reconnect with her family. You might take her along to the store when you go to buy the replacement toy and then let her give the toy to her brother when she comes home. Small actions like this teach children how to maintain connections.

4. *Fix:* Your daughter will need support to fix whatever damage she caused that led to her banishment. If she's been collecting coins or has a little birthday money left over, a dollar toward the purchase price of the new toy would help her to feel (and show her how) she can make a direct contribution to fixing her mistake.

5. *Embrace:* Your daughter will need your embrace and an offer of forgiveness. Her behavior is as much a plea for attention as an attempt to destroy her little brother. Next time there is a birthday celebration in the family, what if she

helped baked the cake? How can she, as the older sibling, feel responsible for her brother's welfare? She'll need to feel a part of the family and some one-on-one time to heal whatever emotional wounds she's feeling.

When we and our children follow these steps, the results are generally very good. Though parents are the ones our children most want to help them fix their messes, in a pinch, as Rhonda's story shows, other adults will do just as well.

Saviors

Show me a crime involving a youth, and I'll show you frayed connections, a young person who has never seen himself or herself as a part of the community. The child may be a loner or may associate with other youth who feel just as excluded. Together, young people who exist on the margins of their communities' or their families' emotional spaces reinforce each other's antisocial patterns. It's difficult to prevent their problem behaviors when they grow up in societies that don't hold them accountable, ask of them a contribution, or offer them a proud part in maintaining the emotional fabric of daily life.

Unfortunately, children's saviors must sometimes be found among the professionals paid to help them. Shane Dunphy describes these children in his moving chronicle of his twelve-year career as a child and youth-care worker on the front lines of practice in Ireland.[14] He was often the only line of defense between children and their abusive, neglectful, alcoholic, and emotionally damaging parents. Dunphy's stories, at their core, are about severed connections and abandonment. He offers the children on his caseload a relationship with a positive, caring adult who won't abuse them or leave them when times get tough, a worker they can count on for a hug when they need one.

A loving relationship is often all our children want. However, it's better when the savior is an extended family member or even a volunteer or professional like Dunphy, as these adults tend to be less transient.

With practically no money, Brian Henry and other volunteers work with the Toronto Catholic School Board to get kids reconnected with school. Henry knows what kids need. His own history is one of gangs and prisons, poor school attendance, and trouble at home. The organization he founded, HOODLINC, handpicks a group of grade nine students and provides them with a special classroom where the student numbers are kept low. Volunteers go to their homes and drag them out of bed if they don't come to class. Through their every action, the adults let the kids know they care about these young teens and understand the odds stacked against them. These are thirteen- to fifteen-year-olds with records, most from fatherless homes that Henry describes as "survival units" with young moms just barely getting by. Peter Barrans, the principal of the special academic unit that houses HOODLINC, insists that it's consistency that counts when it comes to reengaging the kids. Numbers, too. There is something about the connection you get when you have just eight students and one teacher. As Barrans explains, "When I'm in a class of twenty-two, I teach science. When I'm in a class of eight, I teach students."

Take these connections away, and you have the perfect environment in which to raise a psychopath. Just ask any child soldier. Traumatize a child with violence and separation from his parents, submit him to fear and make him do things he knows better than to do (maiming others, cannibalism, incest, burning property, murder), and you slowly strip away the glue that creates sociability. Emotionally numb, a child will want to do anything to feel connected again, even if that means taking up arms against his own people. He will do anything to feel a part of a community, to feel as if he belongs and has a contribution to make. He will attach to anyone who offers to protect him.

These days, I have come to think of children as dry sponges, just waiting for someone to saturate them with a warm embrace. I feel a kinship with heroes of mine, like Stephen Lewis, the UN secretary-general's special envoy for HIV/AIDS in Africa, who has written about his many visits to impoverished communities across that continent. In Kigali, Rwanda, he met with a couple hundred schoolchildren and their caregivers. He dutifully listened to the women tell him about their problems after the genocide a decade earlier, problems only made worse by the spread of AIDS. These women told Lewis about the orphans they must shelter and feed, the lack of food, their own grief over having lost so many of their adult children. But stories of hundreds are difficult to make sense of. They seldom move us as much as the story of one. Lewis writes about that meeting most passionately when he shares his memory of a little girl with unkempt hair and piercing green eyes. When he had finished speaking with the women, he found her standing close to him amid the crowds: "I suddenly felt a tiny figure tuck itself into my body, so close, so tight, it was as if we were welded one to the other."[15]

Give a child a chance to connect, and she will. Offer a child a savior who embraces her, and she will open her heart.

Tips List

There are many ways parents show their children that they really count. Touch and an appreciative gaze come in many forms. Here are some ways parents can help cement a family together.

- Never underestimate how much your children want time with you. Give back some time to your family whenever you can.
- Take all your annual vacation. Being around opens up opportunities for spontaneous sharing.
- Have dinner together at least three times a week. Study after study shows this to be among the simplest and most profound ways to create family cohesion.
- Have a family meeting once a month. Start by asking everyone what was the day's least and most favorite part. Then take some time to plan a family event and discuss problems that affect everyone.
- Tell your children at least once a week, "I appreciate what you did."
- Ask your children what they think they do well. Then have them show you how they do it.
- Ask your children to help when help is needed. Even when a parent becomes ill, there is an opportunity for children to rally around and be helpful.
- Avoid hypocrisy. It poisons an atmosphere of honesty and respect, which is the foundation of good family functioning.
- Move the television out of the family room, and put it someplace where it is uncomfortable to watch! At least for a few months, make the family room a comfortable place to read, play games, do homework, and talk.

chapter five

The Best and Worst of Connections

Meaghan came to see me at the urging of her mother, who was worried her daughter was depressed. It had all started when Meaghan's friend, Natia, became quite ill with anorexia nervosa and was hospitalized. As if that weren't bad enough, Natia had escaped from the hospital and had run to Meaghan's house, where she raided the family's medicine cabinet and overdosed on Meaghan's mother's painkillers left over from a back operation. Natia had had her stomach pumped. Within days, Meaghan was back at the hospital to see Natia, feeling guilty for having failed to protect her friend.

Meaghan is the type of fifteen-year-old kid who draws people to her. She's pretty, with big brown eyes and an engaging smile. She has never wanted for friends or attention from boys. Natia liked hanging out with Meaghan. It felt safe having someone like Meaghan around.

"So where would you like to begin?" I asked Meaghan once she'd settled into her seat in my office. It was warm. The heat was up again in our building, and I'd had to open the window even though there was snow outside. Meaghan didn't seem to mind the heat. She sat with her coat on the entire time we spoke, as if ready to bolt if I said anything against her or her friend.

"Tell you what happened?"

I nodded.

"A few weeks ago, my best friend tried to kill herself. She was already in treatment for anorexia. She looked really awful. She even told me she'd hinted to her therapist at the hospital that she was going to do something. I guess I am the only one who really understands her. You know, who knows how serious she can be."

"Has she told you things like this before?" I asked. Natia had. The summer before, Meaghan had helped take Natia to the hospital. Natia was threatening to cut her wrists. The staff at the hospital didn't do much about it at the time.

"That's what got me so upset, because her mom came home a few days later to find her on the floor of her room, and she'd slashed her wrists and really tried to kill herself. How could they not see it? I thought they were trained to know these things."

I could tell Meaghan hadn't gotten over the shock of her friend's first suicide attempt. It's no coincidence that when children know someone who has attempted suicide, they are at a much greater risk of attempting suicide themselves. Meaghan's own depression was making sense.

It can be confusing to be confronted by another's pain and the hopelessness of knowing there is little one can do except offer one's support. I think Meaghan was telling me her world fractured a little that day. Suddenly adults weren't quite as dependable as they were supposed to be.

"I went in and saw her that night at the hospital," Meaghan told me with tears now misting her eyes. "And she was really tired, and I felt all these what-ifs. Like what if her mom hadn't come just then, or what if the hospital hadn't discharged her. And what if I had done something else. It's put a lot of stress on my shoulders. But I'm responsible for her. She's my friend. Well, actually more. I'm the only non-family member who gets to visit Natia any time she wants me there. We're that close."

It seemed that Meaghan was doing exactly what we'd want all our children to do for their friends: be supportive during a crisis.

"That sounds wonderful. Like you were being a great friend," I said.

"Yeah, I was. Only then, everything got real crazy. You see, one of the girls on the unit at the hospital was sneaking in drugs. Heroin.

"And she was asking Natia to get her needles. Then getting Natia to try it. So then Natia began to ask me to get the needles. She said the other girl might beat her up if I didn't help. She sort of looked scared. So I asked my mom what to do, and she said we had to call the hospital. And we did. I had to. I was responsible for her, and I couldn't let her do it. But Natia was real angry with me. They met with the girls on the unit and did these searches and threatened to send them into a secure detox if they found drugs. And then Natia called me that night and was yelling at me about it."

The more intense the situation became, the more Meaghan's world became a dark place.

"You did everything you could," I told her. "More than most friends would do. Natia may one day see that." My voice was very quiet so that she wouldn't be frightened by what I was saying. Meaghan had acted compassionately, but what she hadn't understood is that reaching out still means maintaining personal boundaries. It's something professional counselors learn early in their careers, and then relearn every day they practice. Meaghan was just a kid trying to play an adult role. She'd done reasonably well, but had become too enmeshed emotionally. Natia's success and failure were becoming Meaghan's, too.

"I feel like I just wanted to shake her," she said. "It makes me so sad that she doesn't understand what she is doing to everyone else. Like she's in there wasting her time. She won't try. She won't get well. She's hurting herself, and she doesn't even know it."

"And she's hurting you, too? Does it feel like that?" I asked.

"Yeah. Sort of. It's like everyone else is doing the worrying for her."

Somewhere in Meaghan's mind, her well-being and Natia's had become jumbled together. I told Meaghan, "You've done so much for your friend, but sometimes all we can give is a secure space to heal. Natia has to do her own healing. She has to want to heal. I don't know if you can rush that."

Meaghan listened, then began to cry.

"It's your job to be there for her," I explained after I'd handed Meaghan a box of tissues. "But it's Natia's job to make decisions for herself."

It was a complicated message for a young girl confused by her first experience with such strong emotions. No matter how well we have been loved, sharing ourselves with another brings with it the risk of our own vulnerability. Many parents I work with become concerned when their teenagers sacrifice themselves for the benefit of another, sometimes a boyfriend or girlfriend, sometimes a parent or grandparent. Our kids are seldom balanced in their convictions. They want, even need, to throw themselves wholeheartedly into the role of savior. One can feel so grown-up taking responsibility for another.

Emotional Touches

Most children who themselves have experienced a strong emotional connection with another person will survive these first traumatic exposures to others' pain. Children survive when their relationships remain constant. In Meaghan's case, her friendship with Natia was a rite of emotional passage of her own choosing.

A well-loved child like Meaghan, a member of the We Generation, will feel compelled to reach out to others in need. She will seek not only physicality, but also emotional connections and spiritual bonds. Children of the We Generation want all three:

1. The physical touch that tells them they matter
2. The emotional connections that help them attune to others' feelings
3. A sense of spirituality that brings with it feelings of belonging and purpose

When these connections are denied them, children can always find alternatives that are more troubling.

Touched Sexually

Without easy access to touch, physical or emotional, our children are likely to seek the warmth they miss in whatever ways they can. In Heather O'Neill's novel *Lullabies for Little Criminals*, we meet Baby (that is really her name, she tells us), a twelve-year-old prostitute on the streets of Montreal, raising herself while her drug-addicted father tries his best to look after himself. O'Neill shows us through her fiction just how a neglected child can use sex to secure substitute attachments. Baby does better than we might expect, even if she falls into the sex trade and is badly exploited by everyone she thinks is her friend. Tragically, she finds the love she is looking for in the most distressing of ways.

There are youngsters who never live the life of the street worker but whose sexual connections make them just as vulnerable to exploitation. Fourteen-year-old Naomi dates men ten years older than her. She tells me it's because they act like fathers to her. They make her feel safe. They touch her in nice ways. She admits the sex stuff means very little. She likes the intimacy, though, and the gifts, and being there at her boyfriend's side. She says she feels important when she's with him, much older, secure.

Can we really blame Naomi for confusing sex and intimacy? Her solution to finding touch may repulse us, but can't we understand her need? After all, adults make the same mistake, using sex to find intimacy. What I want the young people with whom I work to experience is the right to make an informed choice about their bodies. I want them to find substitutes for sex that make them feel just as intimately connected to others as they might feel when sexually active.

There is a difference between the child driven to sexual activity out of desperate need and the child who is simply experimenting with her newfound body and feelings. The explorer will not be manipulated. The well-coached explorer is more likely to act responsibly and keep herself safe. The desperate child, however, is a target for exploitation.

Teens are particularly vulnerable. Suddenly, sex is a viable alternative to touch. It's somewhat biochemical; sexual activity produces oxytocin, a hormone that induces feelings of relaxation, happiness, and contentment. Oxytocin makes us addicted to another's touch.

Sex offers children an easy way to feel connected and content. Many make that choice. Studies of sexual activity among youth have shown consistent patterns for decades. Our kids today are no more sexually active than we were at their age some twenty, thirty, or forty years ago.[1] Most careful surveys of young people show that when it comes to sexual activity involving intercourse:

- 10 percent of eighth graders are sexually active;
- 20 percent of ninth graders are sexually active;
- 30 percent of tenth graders are sexually active;
- 40 percent of eleventh graders are sexually active;
- 50 percent or more of twelfth graders are sexually active.[2]

The surprising news is that those numbers have been decreasing for the past decade, especially among some high-risk groups of youth such as the urban poor. Nor are the numbers skewed by children simply substituting other sexual behaviors such as oral sex. Despite the hoopla in our popular media, community epidemiologists who study these things are not finding huge increases in the number of children engaged in any form of sexual activity as compared with generations before them.

The fact is, like their parents, today's youth use sex to connect and jump the maturity gap. "It feels good," kids say. I would rather concentrate my attention on helping children find alternatives to early sexual initiation than endlessly preaching at them "No!" "Wait!" or "Abstain!" If those messages were ineffective when their parents were growing up, I doubt they are going to be heard in an age of MTV and low-slung jeans.

What will work is ensuring our children are connected to their families and communities. Just as it's ludicrous to expect a hungry child to ignore a plate of hot food placed in front of him, it is equally absurd to tell a disconnected child to abstain from sexual intimacy.

What I've learned from the kids themselves is that the children with the largest social webs of friends, the most consistent and nurturing attachments to parents, and adult-size responsibilities in their communities are the children the least likely to feel the need to become sexually active early in order to feel connected.

The Dating Substitute

Of course, even the most well connected young person is still going to think about sex and want to explore her sexuality, no matter what her religious background or household values. Teenage pregnancy knows few class, race, ethnic, or religious barriers.

We might mythologize our own puritanical pasts, but moral blindness won't change our children's desire to touch, to experiment, and to experience their bodies. Elvis shocked us with his swinging hips. We grossed our parents out with the Rolling Stones *Sticky Fingers* album. Then there was *Grease,* punk, and transsexual glam rock bands like Kiss. Sure, it all seems so funny now, but think back to the outrage at the time. Now we have Britney Spears's suggestive videos, and groin-swiveling dances in junior high that have led some schools to cancel the events altogether.

When is too much connection too much? When do our children cross the boundaries of decency?

I'm not sure I have the answer, but I am not going to condemn the kids for doing exactly what we adults did. Different look, same chaos. Our kids want what we had. A way to explore their sexuality, to gently rebel. It is all so . . . inevitable.

If we think we can stop it, we are fooling ourselves. What we can do is offer our children opportunities to connect in ways that hold the promise of intimacy without the danger of carelessness.

Prevention Works

Programs that prevent children from becoming victims to unwanted touches begin early. Hundreds of national initiatives have helped children understand the difference between good touch and bad touch, and they share some important lessons with parents, too:

- *Bad touch is different from good touch:* Most schools are at least talking about bullying and intimidation. Most coach kids to "tell someone you trust if someone makes you feel uncomfortable." Those are messages

---

many of us a generation or two ago didn't hear very often, if at all. Good prevention programs promote discussion. They tell kids, "Tell someone if something bad happens"; "Trust your feelings"; "It's not your fault when someone hurts you." Our children today have a much better understanding of good and bad touch than we did when we were kids.

- *Hear it thrice:* The best way to prepare our kids to know the difference between good touch and bad is to make sure they hear the explanation more than once. Three times is better than twice, and ideally, there is time between the tellings for the children to grow and put what they're learning into practice. The most effective abuse-prevention programs reinforce the same messages from one grade to another. It's an approach the RespectED program of the Red Cross of Canada uses. Initiated by Judi Fairholm in Vancouver two decades ago, this program provides youth in grades six and seven with a multiweek program of exercises and videos, delivered by volunteers, that teach the students about abuse, whom to tell, and how to keep themselves safe. That program, called It's Not Your Fault, is followed up a few years later, when youth in grade nine participate in a program called What's Love Got to Do with It? The themes are revisited, this time emphasizing age-appropriate lessons on dating and dating violence.

- *Say what you mean, and mean what you say:* If you mean penis, say penis. If you mean breasts, say breasts. If you mean intercourse, say intercourse, and make sure your child understands the plumbing. Preventing our children from abuse and promoting healthy touching doesn't happen when we mystify children's bodies. Make the body a strange, unknowable thing, and you can bet the kids are going to go exploring. I'd rather they have a map along for the adventure. The best of the prevention programs give kids the language to know what they are talking about and a range of words to describe their feelings.

- *It's a big, complicated mess:* The best prevention programs help kids pull all the messages about touch together. Children's psychosexual development is intertwined with the social challenges they experience on the playground and at home. It's not just that our children begin to feel things; it's that they have to find ways to express themselves. If our preteens and teens sometimes turn into whirling masses of spiteful anger, it's because they are overwhelmed by a maelstrom of competing demands and anxiety over how to behave. We can ease our kids through this by explaining the connections between thoughts, feelings, and behavior: "Acne is partially related to hormonal changes," you'll need to explain, "which are the same hormonal changes that affect your feelings about sex and intimacy. Which will make you want special relationships with other boys or girls, which will mean rejection or acceptance." The words you use shouldn't be so technical, but the content will probably be the same. Try telling your child in plain language what's happening to them: "Your body is changing. That means pimples and, of course, more body hair and all kinds of other changes [be as specific as you can]. You'll start thinking about boys [girls], and that can be a little strange or nice, or both. Your body is going to begin to do things you don't always feel like you control. I know this can be embarrassing, but we all experience these same things growing up. If you have any questions, or need anything, just ask." If you're really brave, you might want to be very specific and open up a conversation about the many perils of growing up: worries about masturbation, wet dreams, and first kisses. There may be feelings of rejection so stinging that thoughts of suicide flicker through your child's mind. Somehow, the pieces will eventually snap together. A nudge in the right direction from a parent, though, never hurts.

Touched by Gangs

When our children don't get our help, they are left to figure out these complicated connections themselves. Gangs grow where kids feel disconnected, when they have no real responsibilities or place in their societies. These groups grow amid unemployment and a lack of strong adult role models to place healthy expectations on young people to make a contribution. They grow when kids are left to figure out adolescence on their own. When bad touches are all kids know.

Middle-class communities aren't immune. Kids who feel disconnected from adults and who are desperate for the security that gang affiliation brings drift into delinquency as a solution to problems they cannot solve alone. That includes violence (it's one way to feel powerful, to control who touches you and how), early sexual activity (sex is a poor substitute for intimacy, but it works nonetheless), drugs (they are an effective way many kids find to numb the overwhelming emotions they feel or to provide recreational distractions when part of a group), and property crime (a way to feel successful among one's peers).

If we are committed to preventing our children from drifting in that direction, we will need to provide them with a better sense of belonging in our families, schools, and communities. Crime suppression units, tougher jail sentences, police in our schools—none of these solutions are going to solve the problem of youth delinquency unless we understand what our kids really want. Crime disappears (or at least drops substantially) when children feel a part of their communities and have the guidance of adults to help them feel connected during a tumultuous time in their development.[3]

Good kids and bad tell me the same thing. They need to be touched. Physically.

After all, touch is the keystone for emotional and spiritual connections.

Spiritual Touches

In the Bamboo Temple ten kilometers inland from the seaside resort of Yantai in eastern China, my thirteen-year-old son Scott and I wander quietly among the Buddhist statues. The view is spectacular, out over a green valley toward the ocean. The architecture has swooping rooflines that end in carvings of ancestral dragons. The monks have retired to their dormitories for the afternoon, having risen before dawn for their prayers. We walk quietly, lighting incense in the uppermost temple hundreds of steps above the entranceway to the grounds. I'm a little surprised when Scott tells me, "In a place like this, you can feel alone."

I admire him for letting the calmness of the setting capture his thoughts. There is a stillness here, as there is in many religious buildings. It invites us to move from our connections with the everyday to thoughts of something more profound.

Not all children have the opportunity to slow down. Many years ago, I led a group of youth in their midteens on a backwoods camping trip. Among the twelve was a young man, François, who had been raised in the city and who had spent much of the previous year abusing drugs or running to the street. His parents had insisted he attend the camp. They thought it would do him some good to get away from the distractions of the city. I had the feeling they thought the camp's primitive conditions might also punish him for behaving badly.

François was a frenetic kid who loved to show off. He didn't mind being at the camp. He liked impressing the other kids with his rudeness. He'd pull down his pants and moon strangers. He'd tell racist jokes. He'd start food fights. I thought with time he might calm down.

I was wrong. While preparing dinner, I had asked François and his tent-mates to gather some firewood. I gave them a small hatchet and a saw. While I was starting the fire with kindling, I could hear in the distance the thwack of wood being chopped. I assumed that the kids were cutting one of the many deadfalls that were all around us. It wasn't until another youth, Kelly, suggested I go see what François was doing that I began to worry. It was a short walk to where I found him, madly hacking away at a beautiful forty-foot white pine that stood majestically at the bend of a river. Its leafy canopy was a lovely intense green against the speckled white bark of the tree. It was too late to save it.

"What are you doing?" I shouted. François grinned. The other youth looked startled, then ashamed.

"Just getting some wood. Like you told us," he said and continued hacking at the tree.

"I appreciate the effort," I said sarcastically. "But why did you have to kill such a beautiful tree? There's already lots of fallen wood."

"I don't know," François shrugged.

I believed him. I don't think he was aware of the impact his actions had on others or the environment. He hadn't considered that the people who next came to our campsite might have enjoyed looking at that magnificent tree. His was a world of impulse. He knew only rules and how to get around them. His connections were the superficial ones of immediate first impressions.

I felt sad for him.

Nor was I able to reach him emotionally or spiritually that summer. He was eventually sent home when he vandalized the property of a nearby village, taking a baseball bat and breaking the caps on a length of fencing that ringed the ball diamond. It was a silly, disrespectful act.

I'm afraid there are some children who need to be forced to slow down, to reflect, to hear the messages of their elders. For children like François, this may come in a drug detox unit or in jail.

The good news is that the other three youths who watched François fell that tree learned something that day. One of those youths, Alan, told me later, "I hadn't thought about what we were doing until you told us to stop. Really. I just didn't think about it. There are so many trees in the forest. Like, what did it matter? But then I saw it. That really was an amazing tree. I sort of feel stupid doing what we did."

Spiritually Connected

We know we are connected to the divine when our spine tingles, our mind is focused, or we feel deeply satisfied. In those moments, the spiritual warms us. It brings connections. It sustains our children more than we may suspect. At least, it can, when spirituality is not forced or threatened. When religion turns spirituality into empty rules and threats stacked one upon the other, it becomes oppressive. Our children abandon the teachings, just as many of us abandoned them.

That's how it was for Jackie. In her twenties now, she has left behind religion. "I just got so tired of being told I was a bad person," she says. "I'm not a bad person. My body isn't evil. The church was getting in the way of my feeling good about myself."

Jackie hasn't abandoned spirituality. She's abandoned the prescriptive rule book of a church that many young people feel they have to reject. Let's face it, most young people aren't ready to write off large numbers of humanity because those others are not following the same religious path as they themselves are following. Those who do aren't thinking We. A We Generation is more likely to see the similarities among religious paths.

The problem with organized religion is it can run counter to the needs of a We Generation. In this more global and interactive world, a religion that preaches exclusion and privilege threatens a We Generation taking root. How can we expect our children to feel connected and responsible for others if we tell them others are evil or ignorant? Pews and prayer mats have much in common. We adults err when we focus on differences. Our Me-thinking runs counter to the enthusiasm young people show for tolerance.

Despite the problems, however, our children can still find in religion a more positive message when heaven is understood as a house with many rooms. Youth often take a liberal view toward what they are being taught in their churches, mosques, synagogues, and temples. Their affiliation with their religious communities gives them a feeling of belonging, even if they don't agree with or absorb everything it teaches.

Religious communities can also be a place of refuge. Rani, a fourteen-year-old refugee who escaped the death threats of her Middle Eastern homeland just prior to September 11, 2001, hasn't found it easy living in the West. She has racial slurs directed at her, especially when she wears her head scarf. By embracing her religion and culture, Rani has coped with her exclusion. She makes no efforts to fit in with other children her age. She is devout in her practice as a young Muslim and is proud to let her family make decisions for her. She attends a school for Muslim children, in a classroom with only girls. Rani's world is safest when she remains separate.

Cloistered in her community, adhering to her religion, Rani feels strongly connected to her family and the small community of other newcomers who look and dress like her. Her religion sustains and protects her, whether she believes in what it teaches her or not. Her identity as a Muslim connects her to a web of support. She thrives despite her exclusion.

Rani's experience is not unique. Study after study has shown that immigrants who do not acculturate often experience better mental health and are happier than those who try to fit in among people who discriminate against them.

I respect Rani for her solution to being excluded. I am, however, uncertain whether Rani will be a part of the We

Generation. Over time, will her strong devotion to one religious path allow tolerance for others? I worry just as much about those boys and girls who taunt Rani with the racist remarks they have heard at home. Are they, with their small-minded prejudices, any more ready to be a part of a We-thinking world?

I wish it were different. I want all children to feel a spiritual connection without their needing to pass judgment on the paths chosen by others. Many young people want the same. They don't want to be bullied into believing what their parents believe. They want to show us adults a better way—to remind us that prophets as diverse as Jesus, Mohammed, and the Buddha have preached messages of peace and neighborly respect. Youth think about these things.

I encourage parents to encourage their children to be critical consumers of religion. A We Generation will be impervious to the pull of tyranny if it learns to question authority. This generation will be less likely than my generation to become the blind followers of zealots.

Right and Wrong Thinking

Most young people have a sense of what's right and what's wrong. They want to connect themselves to the moral majority. Police know this; investigators appeal to a criminal's sense of ethical conduct. We might glamorize tough cops on television, but the truth is, few police use such heavy-handed techniques. Instead, the interrogator tries to understand the "bad apple." Maybe the suspect has had a tough life; maybe he or she was abandoned by a father, had to support a mother, had to make his or her own way in life, never got ahead in school. If the interrogator says to a suspect, "I understand. Maybe what you did makes sense. You've been through a lot. Maybe you were just feeling like you deserved better," more often than not, the criminal confesses. After all, most everyone wants to be invited into the community and understood. Deep down, all but the most disturbed know right from wrong.

The techniques work because they extend compassion to someone in need of understanding. Pemba Chödrön, a Shambhala Buddhist nun and author, talks of the practice of *tonglen*, a meditation practice for cultivating love and compassion. Those who practice it draw the bad energy of others toward them as they breathe, sense it, and then exhale good energy so that others might heal.[4] It is a practice the We Generation understands. Like Natia's friend Meaghan, the child raised with compassion feels compelled to extend that compassion to others.

I am learning that if our children are to experience spiritual connections, they must engage in the following practices:

- *Slow down.* With calmness comes the opportunity to reflect.
- *Experience the diversity of spiritual paths.* Through exposure to others' religions, we learn respect for the many and varied paths to inspiration. We come to appreciate the similarities in how we search for divine connections.
- *Hear the teachings of their elders.* Formal instruction and ceremony and informal mentorship help children understand how spirituality is expressed through our everyday actions.

- *Express themselves.* Children need to be given permission to question the teachings of their elders, so that the young people may better understand those teachings.

Deborah Kimmitt, a Canadian stand-up comedian, says religion is like a Playtex bra: It lifts, then separates. She also says that God was playing the telephone game when he (or she?) shared a few wise words with humanity. A message was whispered, and we all heard just a little different version of the same thing. Such jokes tickle the funny bones of a We Generation.

Our Common Spirit

As M. Scott Peck, psychiatrist and author of *The Road Less Traveled*, eloquently showed readers a generation ago, religion is not just about a God from without, but about a sense of connection within.[5] It's about feeling that we are a part of others' lives and of our culture, and of something bigger than what we see in the mirror. Call that bigger something whatever you like: If one reads broadly, one finds there is more sameness in the scriptures than differences. Sunday hats in church, Muslim scarves and Sikh turbans all cover one's head. The Catholic's bended knees, the Tibetan Buddhist's full-body *kora* (a circumnavigation of a temple one body length at a time), and the Muslim's prostrations all serve to humble. Holy water, holy wine, the cleansing of the body five times a day—is there really much difference? A bus tour of Bethlehem or a pilgrimage to Mecca, paying homage at New York's Ground Zero, the reverence Parisians show at Napoleon's tomb, the wonder inspired by a canoe trip down a river on a crisp autumn day, a climb on Mount Tai Shan in eastern China to honor ancestors . . . The more I travel, the more I am aware of how much our practices share in function, though they differ in form. Places of worship bring communion, with God, community, family, and friends, whatever their guise. Even the atheist is likely to find reassuring the message of peaceful coexistence that the many and varied spiritual shrines embody.

How can we ever expect to raise a We Generation if we don't help our children experience the diversity of spiritual paths? How can we expect our young people to become the caring contributors we want them to become if we promote in them hatred and prejudice? I was stunned by the recent release of a "Christian" video game that glorifies religious violence. Based on a series of books, *Left Behind: Eternal Forces*, is set in postapocalyptic New York, where the player joins a "Christian" organization fighting the forces of the Antichrist, the Global Community Peacekeepers, loosely modeled on the UN Peacekeepers, which "impose" one world government. The warriors kill, then pray and are forgiven for killing. The goal seems to be either to force others to convert, or to kill others for thinking differently.

Parents As Spiritual Guides

As parents, we don't have to take our children halfway around the world to find a sense of spiritual oneness that challenges the small-mindedness of hateful teachings. In almost every community, there is diversity if we look for it. There are Chinese New Year festivals, and Middle Eastern food fairs that follow periods of fasting. There are weekend folk festivals with eclectic mixes of world music that often have spiritual undertones. Most large cities have neighborhoods where one can walk and experience humanity's range of cultural customs, many religion-based. There you'll find incense sticks, prayer flags, meditation bells, and rosary beads. If you're lucky, you'll arrive during a street celebration marking an important holiday. When we look, we can usually find a tasty sample of differences close at hand.

Once our children have slowed down and tried many and varied forms of spirituality, I see a role for their elders to share with them different versions of the "truth." At least then our children will be ready to hear their family's teachings as simply one of many accounts of what makes the world go round. The child who listens with critical ears and is then encouraged to ask questions will eventually be touched spiritually. Parents who worry too much about their child's moral development run the risk of driving them from a spiritual path, away from thinking We.

When Amy was born, her parents made sure they provided everything their daughter would need to grow up successfully. They moved to a good neighborhood. They built a brand-new house. Virla, Amy's mother, vowed to stay at home with her children. Howie, Amy's father, worked long hours, the stress of selling biomedical components taking its toll on his waistline. Meanwhile, the house was kept immaculate. Virla and Howie put down white carpeting throughout their home. The children were made to mind the rules. Virla kept herself busy with her show home. In the garage, Howie had a new Porsche that he polished every weekend.

At times, Amy must have felt she too was another of her mother's pet projects. On the surface, it looked as if Amy's parents were all about her and what she needed. They dressed her in beautiful dresses and took her to synagogue on Saturdays. They ensured she spent summers at expensive camps where campfire songs were sung in Hebrew. When it came time to prepare for her bat mitzvah, Amy was made to dutifully attend every preparatory class. At first she didn't mind. This was her community. These were her friends. She liked having her own history. She enjoyed the traditions, the food at Passover, and the weddings where all the guests seemed to feel they belonged.

It only began to unravel when Amy met Richard at a school dance. They were both sixteen. Richard wasn't Jewish. His parents were . . . well, nothing really. Richard had never attended a church of any kind. But he thought a lot about peace and volunteered at school as a peer mediator, helping to resolve fights between kids on the playground.

If it had just been a casual date with the boy, the whole matter would probably have blown over. Amy would have found her way back to her community. Her parents would have overlooked her interest in the boy as normal teenage curiosity. But Richard and Amy were much more serious than that. Amy had gone to see her family doctor on her own and was on birth control, something her mother found out by accident when she was cleaning her daughter's bathroom. When confronted, Amy stood up for herself. "I can think for myself," she told her parents. "Isn't that what you wanted?"

"No," her father shouted back. "You're too young to be thinking for yourself."

The arguing quickly reached an impasse, and Amy was sent to counseling.

"I like Richard," Amy told me when she was forced to meet with me. "It doesn't matter to me what his religion is. He and I believe the same things." She looked frustrated and close to tears. "My parents only ever tell me what to do. I don't need a shrink to convince me they're right. I know what I'm doing." It was hard for me to argue with Amy. She and Richard were being careful sexually. Amy liked what the boy had to say and the sense of freedom he brought to her life.

"I'm not sure which is worse for your parents," I said. "Is it that you are sexually active or that Richard isn't Jewish?"

"I think it's because he's not Jewish. We know lots of other kids, especially our cousins from Israel. They all do it early. So I don't think my parents have any right to be freaking about that. If Richard was Jewish, they'd totally ignore everything else. I'm sure of that."

Over my career, I've worked with Mormons, Southern Baptists, Muslims, Anglicans, Jews, followers of traditional Aboriginal spirituality, Wiccans. I've lived and traveled in two dozen countries. I've walked the hallowed cliff caves of Buddhist monks, been awed by Istanbul's Blue Mosque, watched the devout in front of Jerusalem's Wailing Wall, been enchanted by drumming circles, and felt the peace of Paris's Notre Dame Cathedral. It's hard to imagine a single version of the "truth" when the divine is honored in so many compelling ways. In Amy, I saw a curious young woman who was listening with her heart. I could understand her parents' fear. There is a long history of assimilation of Jews and, with it, the risk of losing faith and community. Unfortunately, the more Howie and Virla held their daughter back from her friends, the more likely it was that she would never return to Judaism as her faith.

"We're not saying she can't date the boy, but this, well, this is all far too serious. She could at least date some Jewish boys for once. Is that too much to ask?" Virla said during one of our family meetings.

"I'm not sure what's right or wrong here. I hear you want your daughter to keep a connection to her faith. Can we agree on that?"

"Yes," Howie said.

"Then maybe we could find a way to give Amy some say over who she dates, but still expect her to participate in your community's traditions just the same."

It was a compromise that worked remarkably well. Amy still loved her cultural heritage. She was more than willing to help with food preparation and participate in the celebration of holidays. She was pleased to continue to be a part of her synagogue's youth group, even coaching the younger children during Hebrew lessons. As long as she didn't have to give up her relationship with Richard.

Eventually, she and Richard parted ways. "That sex thing," Amy told me, "was way overblown." I could read between the lines. She'd wanted Richard for his ideas. He'd perhaps wanted her for something else. Some things are the same in all cultures.

Amy's next boyfriend wasn't Jewish. But by then, Amy was looking at a move to university. She was seriously considering the University of Haifa in Israel. Her parents were ecstatic when they heard, but they held back from making too much noise about the whole thing. Behind Amy's back, they told everyone. To their daughter's face, all they said was, "Are you sure?"

"I know they're bullshitting me," Amy told me when we met one day on the street. "I know they really want me to go. And I do, too. It will be fun to visit my roots."

A Life-Sustaining Sense of Connection

The dogmatic teaching of the *Left Behind* books and the video game is an anachronism, a leftover from a past that raised selfish children who start wars. The future belongs to children like Amy. Youth who understand how they fit in, in a world that is connected.

I am buoyed by the work of people like Joanna Macy, an ecophilosopher and activist who says we are at a "great turning."[6] Macy takes the long view of our responsibilities to each other. Hers is a plan for a We Generation. Recognizing that modern humans have only been running around this globe for 10,000 generations, Macy challenges us to think about what we are leaving the next 10,000 generations. She takes aim at the selfishness of the "industrial growth society." Macy argues growth is simply not endlessly possible. Mathis Wackernagel and William Rees, among the best known of environmentalists, spoke years ago about the concept of each person's having an "ecological footprint."[7] How large a landmass do we each need to sustain our lifestyles? Estimates are that if every person on earth enjoyed the same standard of living as the average North American, we would need 4.7 earths to have enough minerals, energy, and living space.

Macy says we need to shift to a life-sustaining society. That change would be a revolution in how we understand ourselves spiritually—a change that compels us to think about the needs of others and our environment. It is a revolution our children seem to be comfortably embracing. This third revolution, following the agricultural revolution and the industrial revolution, is an ecological revolution. It is founded on the principle of sustainability, which really means that each of us today, and tomorrow, should be certain we will be cared for. As Macy tells us, "It is our birthright to live on this planet without thinking we're running ourselves to ruin." Judging by our children's enthusiasm for waste management and ecological projects, it seems they are learning about the need for some "radical interdependence." That's We-thinking in action.

One can't ignore that the environmental revolution is infusing our children with a sense of connectedness to both people and planet. While François, cutting down the magnificent white pine, may not have understood this kind of interdependence, the others watching him did, at least when they were challenged to calm down, think, and ask questions.

There is an Aboriginal saying, "All things are connected." Thich Nhat Hanh, the Zen Buddhist master who has taught people in the West to become mindful of their actions and thoughts, reminds us, "When you love, if your love is true, you begin to see that the other person is a part of you and you are a part of her or him."[8] That's the new kind of thinking a We Generation is drawn to. "Peace," Thich Nhat Hanh explains, "is the absence of separation, of discrimination. . . . In order to build a community, you have to build yourself at the same time. The community is in you and you are in the community."

The making of a We Generation depends on what adults teach. Maybe Amy was right to rebel, at least just a little. Would we have done any different at her age? Maybe her parents needed to be reminded of something more important than separation and the dogmatism of eternal truths.

Our children are forever influenced by what we share with them and how we live our lives. Tolerance is a learned quality and something we can teach. For example, if you can afford it, live simply for a year and then take the extra cash and travel. Do your kids a favor; show them the world as it really is in all its diversity. Along the way, they'll learn what it means to be connected globally. They'll see their place within a larger world. They'll feel touched and be more willing to reach out to others. Physically, emotionally, and spirituality, they'll be much better off.

Tips List

Children appreciate the efforts parents make to model spiritual connections. That means showing children how to experience a genuine bond with those around them. Many acts of kindness help children develop a life-sustaining pattern of We-thinking behavior:

- Encourage children to spend time with their extended family.
- Organize play dates where there are different ages of children so that your child can both help younger children and be helped by older ones.
- Recognize the wealth of family and community relationships.
- Encourage children to spend an hour a week with the family at a place of worship, whether it is a church, a synagogue, a mosque, the outdoors, or another place that holds spiritual or contemplative meaning.
- Invite all the family members to make a list of what they are thankful for and share it with each other.
- Invite to dinner family friends and neighbors. Doing so will help your children feel part of an interdependent community.
- Rather than complaining about a teacher, a coach, or a referee, ask your child, "What did you do? What was your part in the problem?" Your children will learn to understand the part they play in making their community work rather than blaming others.

- Appreciate another's garden or painted mailbox. Notice something special about another person whom your child knows in the extended family or community.
- Learn that everything is not always fair!
- Encourage children to be more inclusive of those who are excluded in their classroom; suggest your children make sure these excluded kids are included in activities and games.
- Break down stereotypes of race, gender, and sexual orientation by talking about differences positively.
- Ask a child to consider, "How do you think what you just did made him feel?"
- Be honest about people you know and the challenges they face (like a mental illness).
- Model compassion by asking no questions and making no judgments when your child asks for help with a situation that embarrasses him or her.

chapter **six**

An Invitation to Responsibility

"When you do what I've asked, then I'll do what you've asked," a mother of three boys tells her sons, who are aged eight, ten, and twelve. "It's the only way I manage to keep them in line," she explains. "They need to know they have responsibilities, not just to me, but to others, besides."

She's not so different from the store owner down the street from where I live whose windows were vandalized by two thirteen-year-old girls. He was invited to attend a community justice forum, during which the girls and their families, along with the arresting police officer and a teacher who provides the girls with remedial English instruction, met in a church hall over doughnuts and coffee. The girls fidgeted and shrank down on their chairs as the community volunteer, a middle-aged man with a bushy beard and business suit, read the charges. The damage was described in great detail, and the cost of repairs. The girls' choices were made clear. Correct their mistake, or go to court. The store owner, a man in his sixties, kindly agreed to let the girls work for him as their restitution. "They're just kids," he said. "They'll learn." His optimism was infectious.

On the university campus where I teach, a political party is working hard to get youth to participate in an upcoming election. Its slogan is as simple as it is profound: "I vote." Green buttons adorn young people's backpacks on election day. The party doesn't win, but the party that does begins to pay more attention to issues important to those who carry backpacks rather than briefcases.

These small episodes in which invitations to responsibility are offered and accepted by young people remind me of the role we adults play in raising responsible kids who are capable of showing compassion for others. When I look for signs of this compassion, I can find them all around me. Though sometimes hidden amid the blur of our hurried lives, the compassion is there all the same. Stop and look, I remind myself.

When I do, I see a boy in his late teens doing the unexpected. I'm standing across the street from a large apartment block one cold morning in March, waiting for my dog to sniff at the base of a tree. A spring thaw the day before left walkways covered in slush that froze into icy patches overnight with the temperature's sudden plunge. I'm sure the boy has no idea how intently I am watching as he runs toward the building's door, then stops to notice the elderly woman he just bounded past. She is navigating her way up the slippery set of steps leading into the building. I wonder if she is as surprised as I am when the boy turns and offers her his hand, which she takes, gingerly at first; then, as the steps become more treacherous, she is forced to lean on him more intensely. Her dependence on the boy must have taken him by surprise, because his own sneakers slip a little, but the two of them lean toward one another and slowly make their way past the building's glass doors.

The boy's gesture makes me think about young people and their thirst for responsibility. Standing there, it occurs to me that despite all our fears about a generation gone wild, the kids we are raising today are thinking about others more often than we suspect. We need to give, and take, some credit where credit is due. After all, someone sometime must have shown that boy what it means to care for others. To my mind, that someone deserves a prize. That someone must have connected with that boy. Not a digitalized, over-the-Web, instant-messaging sort of connection, but good old-fashioned being there. I'm inclined to believe that's why he acted so responsibly.

Expect the Best from Our Kids

When we offer our children the chance to think We, they are much less likely to turn into the rotten kids we all fear. As one mother of a teenage boy cried, "He's always on the computer or watching television or on the phone. He never talks to my husband and me anymore. It's like having a boarder in the house, a rude boarder. I can't even get him to come to the dinner table or walk the dog. Nothing. I can't stand it. I just want some respect!" It needn't be like that if we insist our kids be part of their families and then back up our words with action. If the dog needs walking, then the dog gets a walk. No ifs, ands, or buts.

In my house, dinner isn't served until the dog gets walked. And you can bet that if I'm knocking myself out getting dinner ready, it's not going to be me doing the walking. Or paying the children to do it! In our house, allowances are never paid for chores that are a reasonable part of a child's contribution to the family welfare. After all, I don't get paid to cook or clean, and to my mind, my children shouldn't, either. My children do get an allowance, but that money is paid to help them learn about managing money responsibly. It's there for them to buy birthday presents and save for something extra they want or need. They do chores, however, because they have responsibilities for others.

Of course, I am keenly aware that I am doing my child no good when I don't hold her accountable. Walking the dog isn't just about giving Rover a run. It's about telling our children, "You are a part of this family," "You belong here," and "We count on you!"

Our kids want these real connections. Whether at our dinner tables or in our basements programming the personal video recorder, our children want an important role in their families—a role that says something powerful about their capacities. They want to feel responsible for themselves and others.

When we let them avoid responsibility, we undermine them by keeping them from finding the thing they want most: a self-description as adult. It is up to us to provide our kids opportunities to show compassion and to be appreciated for the uniqueness of the gifts they have to offer. Like every generation before them, today's young people want to look in the mirror and recognize themselves as responsible young people on the path to maturity.

To Play or to Work?

Tragically, many young people don't experience being needed and aren't held accountable for their actions by their parents.

At sixteen, Torin can shirk his responsibilities and suffer no consequences. It's a little surprising, given the backgrounds of his parents. Torin's father, Jackson, is a self-made man. Barely having finished high school, Jackson has still managed to build his own business trimming trees and landscaping. He handles a chainsaw as easily as he would a safety razor. Torin's mother, Gwen, has a bakery in their basement. She supplies pies and bread to local restaurants and on Saturdays takes her baked goods to the farmers market. She sells out every time.

With parents like these, it was strange to hear that Torin was acting so irresponsibly. He wasn't doing his homework. His parents suspected he was using his allowance to buy drugs. The rumor was that he was not just buying his own drugs, but also buying them for others. It seemed as if Torin had decided that being popular was better than being smart.

It was a short-term strategy with long-term consequences. At parent-teacher interviews in February, the news was sobering. Either Torin would have to work harder, or he would be remaining in grade eleven for another year. Torin shrugged when he heard the news. Afterward, when his father began to curse, Torin agreed to do his homework. It was an empty promise. By the time the daffodils were poking their way through the spring snow, Torin's marks had slipped and he was seldom seen at home.

It was a warm April day, the kind of day when puddles form from the rapid runoff of the melting piles of accumulated winter snow, when I met the family for the first time. I could tell that Jackson was wishing he was back at work, rather than in my office with his grumpy son sitting beside him. There was equipment to get ready and customers to see. Instead, he was listening to Torin complain that this was all a waste of his time.

By our third meeting, not much had changed. The only difference was Torin was now being more belligerent. "I need some money," he kept saying. His friends were all planning a big year-end bash and were going to take in a concert a two-hour drive away. It wasn't going to be a cheap adventure. The tickets were almost eighty dollars, and Torin had practically no money left in his bank account. "You can't expect me to be left out. They're my friends," Torin said, knowing his parents didn't like to hear that their boy was left out of anything. Both Jackson and Gwen knew what it felt like to be overlooked at school. Both had spent years establishing themselves in their community. I stayed quiet, wondering just how excluded Torin would feel next year if he didn't pass grade eleven. I couldn't help but think that maybe missing that concert might make Torin realize what was really at stake.

Jackson figured this might be an opportunity to help his son grow up. "Fine," he said. "Saturday, you can help me get my equipment ready. You can come down to the shop and earn the money." Something in the way Torin smiled made me doubt that this was going to go as planned.

When we met two weeks later, Jackson didn't even bother showing up. Torin sat staring at his unlaced sneakers. Gwen said that the Saturday following our last meeting hadn't gone so well. Torin had been late getting out of bed. He'd eventually walked over to his father's shop, where he was asked to help wash equipment and stack bricks. He worked the first hour, then lost interest. Jackson found him out back listening to music. "I was just taking a break," Torin shouted, the earbuds from his MP3 player still in. That wasn't how Jackson saw it. "I'll work with you, how about that?" he suggested. Torin agreed, but soon enough, the teen said his hands hurt, and the next thing Jackson knew, the boy was sitting and watching while his father did the work. By lunchtime, Jackson suggested that Torin go home.

"What happened with the concert?" I asked, hopeful that Torin might have learned something just the same.

"Oh, we gave him the money," Gwen said. "I know we shouldn't have, but it was the last time he might be with all his friends. We just couldn't say no."

I sympathized with Gwen. No doubt, Jackson hadn't come to our session that day, because he was embarrassed. They both loved their son so much. They both hung on the hope that if he stayed connected with his peers, he would want to pass grade eleven and advance with them. But Torin never did pass grade eleven. He wouldn't realize what had happened until it was too late. His behavior deteriorated further the next year. He became even more reckless and irresponsible. He refused to come to counseling. Soon Gwen stopped attending, too. "Since we started seeing you," she said, "things have gotten worse."

I took the criticism to heart. I reviewed my case notes and thought about what went wrong. Two loving parents and one irresponsible kid. If I were to do it all again, I'd probably work less with Torin and more with Jackson and Gwen. If there was a problem with the work we'd done together, it was forgetting how important parents are to their teenagers when teaching them about responsibility. The feelings of failure that Jackson and Gwen felt during their own adolescence inhibited them from developing reasonable expectations of Torin. In their expression of compassion and in their desire to keep their connection with their son, they had forgotten that responsibility must be forged in the fires of natural consequences.

We Can Nurture Responsibility

I'm not convinced Torin got what he really wanted, either. Sure, he got to go to the concert. And he might convince himself he never really cared whether he passed grade eleven. But that's not what I hear from kids who fail. Most teens tell me, whether from their jail cells or from the streets, that they want someone to hold them accountable. To show them they are worth giving a damn about. Even delinquent adolescents want their parents to be a part of their lives and set some limits. If we expect our teens to join the We Generation, we are going to have to teach them responsibility.

When tears flow and anger spews, I hear young people talk about how important their relationships are with parents, grandparents, teachers, coaches, mentors, bus drivers, store clerks, and employers. These relationships are the clay from which they fashion their identity. "Tell me who I am," they plead. The actions of adults tell kids who they are. That Saturday afternoon in April, Jackson told his son he wasn't man enough to have anyone expect anything of him. When Gwen slipped Torin the money for the concert ticket, she told him he would be her baby forever.

It doesn't have to be like this. Children like Torin may be fridge-raiding, wired, curfew-breaking young radicals, but they still want us to hold them accountable. They want to look up into our eyes and be convinced that we care enough to expect great things of them. They need us to show them that like Charles Dickens, we too believe that "a day wasted on others is not wasted on one's self."

Torin was asking his parents for something far more important than eighty dollars. I think he wanted to hear someone say, "We love you too much to buy you that ticket. We expect more than that of you."

The message we convey should always be "Yes."

"Yes, we expect you to become an adult and assume adult responsibilities."

"Yes, you can count on us to help you reach that goal."

"Yes, we will keep you safe in the meantime."

"Yes, we will provide you the structure you need to grow up at a healthy pace."

A deep sense of connection with others comes from the realization we are all dependent on each other for our well-being. Love is not unconditional giving. It is showing our children we understand what is best for them. It is holding them to account for their actions. It is expecting them to act compassionately toward themselves and others.

As parents, though, we get distracted from what our goal should be.

I was recently called to an early-season meeting of parents whose thirteen-year-old sons are part of a Tier 1 city soccer team. We stood as a group, twenty-five of us, turned with our backs against the cold north wind that was blowing across the open field. Our sons, who had just finished playing, sat on the bleachers next to us or stretched out on the artificial turf at our feet. The coaches explained how important our support would be to the team's success. They needed volunteers to keep everyone informed by e-mail of upcoming games and practices. They needed someone to get water bottles filled before each game. They needed someone else to look after hanging the nets. And of course, we would be responsible for driving our kids to where they needed to be, paying their out-of-town travel expenses, and ensuring that their uniforms were washed and that they showed up with the right-colored socks. I guess sometime in between doing all this, we were also supposed to hold down jobs, cook, clean our homes, maintain our cars, and look after our other children.

Standing there, braced against the wind like Antarctic penguins, I thought to myself, Wait a minute. The busiest people on the field that day were the parents. The least technically competent were the parents. And yet we were being asked to do everything but play. Surely my son, who spends a great number of his waking hours on instant-messaging, was capable of coordinating his practice schedule and that of his teammates? After all, he never seems to have trouble organizing trips to the movie theater or get-togethers in our basement on Saturday evenings. Water bottles? Nets? Ditto. What in God's name were we adults thinking, taking all this responsibility away from our children?

I wish I'd been brave enough to say something there on the field, but I didn't. Those other parents are my friends and neighbors. I couldn't help but think that if I said anything, it would come off as judgmental. I chose instead to change things for my own son, making sure he answered his own e-mails about team practices and travel schedules. Next year, I plan to speak with the coach before the parents meet to explore some new ways of sharing responsibilities.

Benign Neglect Teaches We-Thinking

Think back for a moment. How many of us were raised in homes of benign neglect? Did our fathers and mothers come to every single one of our practices? Did they clear great swaths of time to be sure our water bottles were filled?

That wasn't my experience. I was expected to take responsibility for whatever I could do myself.

When we take away from our children opportunities to act responsibly, we turn them into the self-centered brats whom we loathe. When we understand it is our job to raise responsible children, we are more likely to find teachable moments when we can show our children how to think We instead of Me.

If we stop and think about it, a little more responsibility would help our children

- learn they can be responsible for themselves and others;
- learn the consequences of their actions when mistakes happen (and they will);
- practice being adults (telling us parents what to do, when to have the car ready, when their next game is, and reminding us to put down our trashy novel and get ready);
- learn the life skills they'll need for future employment (time management, people skills, leadership).

I am proud of my son's accomplishments and am happy to drive him to practices and games, carpooling with other parents to make the schedule manageable. I'm just not willing to deny him the opportunity to fill the team's water bottles or coordinate training runs. To do otherwise is to show a lack of compassion for what he needs from me.

Of course, there are limits to our benign neglect. Our job as parents isn't to abandon our children to the wolves of circumstance. It is to coach them through their transition into adulthood. That means gentle reminders. In my son's case, that has meant reminding him, "You haven't told me when the next game is. You'll need to give me at least a day's notice, or I might not be able to drive."

It's hard to watch our children chart these choppy waters on their way to adulthood. Responsibility is dangerous. Our job watching, rather than doing, is never easy. Parenting my children reminds me of century-old homes on the East Coast that were built with a tall, square walkabout poking up through the roofline. It's been called a widow's walk, a place where women would traditionally go to watch the returning fishing boats each evening, hopeful that their husbands would appear in the harbor that day and every day afterward. Tragically, some of those boats never did appear. Houses passed from family to family, and still boats went out and men were taken by the sea.

Most of our children chart far less dangerous waters than the North Atlantic. Our job, though, is no less nerve-wracking . . . to wait for their safe return. Watching our children grow into responsible young people means setting in place love and expectations and then launching the children away from the safe harbors of our homes. If we love our kids, we will wait. We will accept the risks. Waiting is our responsibility.

Raised to Be Compassionate

Jacqueline promises her daughter, Katie, they will go shopping for shoes. The junior high prom is only a week away. Katie has found a dress and booked a time to get her hair done. Jacqueline has been happy to swipe her credit card more than once, helping Katie get ready. It hasn't been easy. The first time Jacqueline went to meet Katie at the mall to buy the dress, Katie called her on her cell phone while Jacqueline was in the store. "We're all getting together at Marley's after school. Sorry, Mom. What about tomorrow?" Jacqueline had left work early to meet Katie and wasn't about to do so again. The next day, she made Katie miss her evening soccer practice so they could go shopping.

"I just couldn't take another afternoon off. I was too busy at work," Jacqueline told me while we sat watching the formal graduation ceremony. "But, my God, she was some angry at me. As if she expected me to drop everything and do just what my little princess wanted." We both laughed at the impertinence of youth. But we both knew our kids get away with irresponsibility because we adults love them to a fault.

"Did she eventually get the dress? The dance is tomorrow, right?" I asked.

"Oh yeah. It's exactly what she wanted. It wasn't too expensive. But, you're not going to believe this, she did it again the next week. She still didn't have shoes for the dress. And so she was insisting we go back to the mall. I guess she just didn't trust herself to buy the right shoes. Well, anyway, you can guess what happened. I got stood up a second time. Tuesday evening, she says she's been invited to a movie. 'Can we go another night?' Which really meant last night, this being Thursday and the prom tomorrow. Well, I'd had it. I told her she could go in her sneakers."

We laughed. I thought Jacqueline was joking. Katie probably thought the same thing.

"I'm serious," Jacqueline said. "It breaks my heart to think she'll have this beautiful gown and she'll have to wear some old shoes, but I've had it. I just don't think she's understanding her responsibility to anyone but herself. It worries me. Like what did I do wrong?"

It can break our hearts as parents to see our children fail, be embarrassed, or rejected. Sometimes, though, when we've done everything possible to be supportive, we show our love by pulling back, extending our child an invitation to responsibility.

Don't expect their thanks. At least not right away. But then, what's the alternative? We nourish the We Generation by holding its members accountable for their actions. Irresponsible behavior must have consequences if we are to convey compassion for our children's true needs. It's a necessary paradox of raising children. Unconditional love without natural consequences won't raise a We-thinking child.

Punishment Versus Discipline

To some, Jacqueline's not buying the shoes for Katie might appear to be punishment. It can certainly feel like that for Katie, but it's not.

Punishment and discipline are two different things. They even sound different. A parent who is yelling at a child is likely punishing the child for making the parent feel uncomfortable. Punishment meets our needs, as authority figures, for control and consequences. Discipline meets the child's needs for accountability and learning. A parent who takes privileges from a child when natural consequences would suffice is punishing where discipline is needed. After all, Jacqueline could have told her daughter, "You're not going to the prom." Far better, though, to let her go with sneakers and to see for herself the consequences of her actions.

It's part common sense, part intestinal fortitude in the face of a child's tears and recriminations. "You don't love me" from your child can stab your heart, which is already hurting from having to deny your child something you'd rather provide.

Don't let your guilt override your common sense.

I prefer discipline strategies that show rather than tell. Offering children reasonable consequences for their actions invites them into the world of responsible adulthood. It tells them, "I respect you too much to save you from your mistakes." It conveys to the young person that he is now old enough to look after some things himself.

Punishment, especially corporal punishment, does not create responsible children or a We Generation. It creates a bunch of conformists who do as they are told and selfishly consider their actions before they do them. Everything becomes about them. Their goal is to avoid punishment rather than to do something right.

The punished child is the child who will steal if he can get away with it.

The punished child will punish others when she is big enough to be another's overlord.

The punished child thinks always about her needs, how she can get what she wants, how she can avoid pain.

A child taught limits, held accountable, given responsibility, and made to fix her mistakes never needs to be demeaned or beaten. That child needs only natural consequences, time-outs, and opportunities to fix what has been broken. Many a child I've worked with in jail has said the worst discipline they've ever experienced was not the slap or kick or hair-pulling of a parent, but the shame associated with facing the victims of their reckless behavior.

Start Young

Raising children to be responsible for others starts from the cradle. If we look at the lives of civil rights activists or those courageous enough to have saved Jews from the death camps when the Nazis controlled Europe, we find that many of those individuals grew up demonstrating caring and compassion for others from a young age. They were taught well. According to John Dovidio, a professor of psychology at the University of Connecticut, and who studies prosocial development in children, "The parents of the rescuers were more caring individuals who were much less likely to use physical punishment to control the behavior of their children. Instead, the rescuers' parents reasoned with their children and explained what their children had done wrong and what kinds of behaviors were expected of them."[1] This kind of treatment teaches children to be considerate of the needs of others.

Barbara Coloroso, in her controversial look at the roots of genocide in *Extraordinary Evil*, speculates that it is a short distance from the entitlement of the bully to the mass murder of those we call "different."[2] It is difficult to imagine a child who is reasoned with and then guided to fulfill the expectations of others ever being complicit in the unthinking harm of others. The earlier we instill in our children a sense of themselves as their brothers' and sisters' keepers, the more likely they are to impress us with acts of courage when they are older.

There is much to be hopeful about in this regard. A generation of children is being raised without corporal punishment. Today's children are being reasoned with and intelligently invited to consider the consequences of their actions. Despite the moral panic of the press, this social experiment is working. Our children are less likely to be criminals today, less likely to be violent.[3] They are, though, more likely to talk back. To challenge authority. To think for themselves. To insist their caregivers be held accountable.

Such freethinking children can be disconcerting for educators who suddenly have a text-messaging, rambunctious, and disorderly group of kids who do not sit in their seats in class. Of course, generations ago, most of those kids wouldn't have been in those seats, anyway. Education was a privilege, and few of our children made it past the lower grades. What did we expect? We now have engaged young people longer in our educational institutions, but we haven't made enough effort to adapt the classroom to suit the needs of this new breed of student.

Where we have successfully experimented with new approaches to education, the results have been wonderful. More group projects and problem-solving assignments have helped teach all students how to collaborate better. For less academically inclined students, alternative courses and structures are making it possible for them to participate in school life and make a contribution. A favorite example of mine is a Prince Edward Island high school where boys and girls who would prefer a hands-on education help build "baby barns" (backyard sheds) that the school then sells to raise funds. These students, often marginalized because of their poor academic performance, have become stars on campus. Together, the members of the class have not only proven they can learn applied mathematics, finance, and project management while increasing their literacy skills, but also raised more money for the school's extracurricular activities than any other single initiative. The results are not just good pedagogically—the school has also created a space where a group of vulnerable students feel they belong and can make a contribution without having to conform to a model of education that failed to meet their needs.

A We Generation Is Taught to Question Authority

The We Generation is not going to blindly accept authority. It is groomed on an Internet culture where everyone is potentially an expert—where Wikipedia lets anyone be an author of knowledge, and where everyone has a right to be heard on YouTube and to tell his or her story on Facebook. Theirs is a more egalitarian world.

At least, it can be. Here in the West, we often wonder how societies like Russia can accept a return to totalitarianism embodied in the leadership of their president, Vladimir Putin. What such failed social experiments teach us is that compassion and good governance need to be taught, transmitted from one generation to the next. The We Generation in the West is a phoenix fashioned from the fires of the 1940s, when grandparents made sacrifices. That phoenix was fattened on the explosion of freedoms in the 1960s, which gave youth a voice. The power oligarchy of age and authority was smashed by freethinking musicians and artists and the everyday behaviors of middle-class youth. We taught the We Generation kids what to think by showing them what we did. Even when we told them to mind their elders, our actions had already spoken louder than words.

It's not the same in societies where young people only know conflict or authoritarianism. China, Iraq, evangelical communities that promote hatred under any guise, all constrain their children's capacities to think compassionately about others. Conflict is a consequence of young people who have been taught by their elders to be small-minded. A stable nation starts at home, watching Mom and Dad in an egalitarian relationship choosing the fabric to reupholster the couch. It grows in a school environment that promotes the democratization of decision making. It is nurtured in communities that offer young people a sense of belonging.

Tips List

In Chapter 1, I suggested creating a box labeled "Tips for Acts of Kindness" and placing it next to the dinner table. Here are some more suggestions to be added to the box. Most are for children, but adults can adapt them for themselves, too.

- Text a thank you note to your mother or father immediately after they drive you somewhere so they know how much you appreciate them.
- Give a friend a chance to use your new toy even while you're still learning how to use it yourself (don't make them wait forever for a turn).
- Participate in a walkathon or another fund-raiser for a charity whose work affects a member of your family.
- Give a compliment to someone who serves you at a fast-food restaurant.
- Do two acts of kindness instead of just one!
- Buy a box of chocolates for someone who doesn't usually get told thanks (like a crossing guard, coach, bus driver, or school cook).
- Bake sugar-free or gluten-free cookies for a child who normally can't eat the treats brought to school by the other children.
- Turn *down* the music to be nice to a neighbor.

- Turn *up* the music to be nice to a different neighbor.
- Load your parents' iPod with songs they'll like.
- Pack your own sports gear.
- Make arrangements yourself to get home from a friend's house (but let your parents know what you're doing).
- Patiently wait your turn.
- Do your own laundry.
- Cook a meal even if it isn't your turn, provided you're old enough.

chapter **seven**

Monster Homes Make Monstrous Children

Kiernan's home is a "modest" 3,145-square-foot starter mansion in a new subdivision just outside Toronto. There are five bathrooms, if you count the one in the basement for the live-in housekeeper. Kiernan, who's thirteen, and his sister, Linda, who's ten, both have their own rooms painted in fashionable pastels. They both have an en suite bathroom, their own computer and television, and, to avoid arguments between them, a gaming station each.

There is a bigger television in the large family room off the kitchen, and another set in the basement recreation room. That's Kiernan's father's "man-cave," as his dad likes to call it.

The living room, with its arched windows, is decorated with fine furniture and looks not unlike the set of a photo shoot for *Better Homes and Gardens*. Martha Stewart would be comfortable here. The kitchen is enormous. The granite counters perfectly complement the stainless steel appliances. The counters are clear of any clutter, of course. The toaster and coffee maker are placed in cupboards below, brought out each time they are needed. There is a table to eat at, just the right size for a family of four. That leaves the formal dining room for Christmas dinners and birthdays. The kitchen table isn't used very much, though. Mostly, the family sits on the bar stools by the island, eating quickly when dinner is made ready by the housekeeper and then leaving for the next scheduled event.

The house sits on a small lot, its footprint all but eclipsing the small garden front and back. The double garage thrusts toward the street. It's hard to know when someone is coming to the front door, because there are few windows looking out over the curving driveway.

Kiernan's window is one of these few. His room is on the second floor above the main alcove. From the window of his bathroom, he can look down the stone walkway and across the paved driveway, out to the sidewalk and over the small ash tree that the area builder planted to make the subdivision leafy and green.

Kiernan was at that window that morning, he tells me, on the day he decided to slash his wrist. He'd read that if you slice crosswise—across the veins—you wouldn't die, the blood clots too quickly. He had a sharp pocket knife he'd been given for his tenth birthday. He'd never used it camping. He'd thought he might, but summer vacations were usually at beach resorts or amusement parks. There were no trees to whittle, just fruit to cut, their flesh softer than his own.

Kiernan decided to cut lengthwise.

After the first touch of blade to skin, he hardly felt the knife. He just stood there at the window. At one point he thought, If someone walks by and they look up at our house, I will stop. He waited ten minutes. No one walked by. There were no children on bicycles. His neighbors were hidden behind their own glass panes.

Kiernan wasn't found until nearly ten hours later. When his father came home and parked in the garage, he had thought himself lucky to have a quiet house. He'd showered, eaten, and then headed to his office, which looks out over the backyard. Kiernan's mother came home two hours later with Linda. They'd been at Linda's gymnastics practice. Kiernan's mother had met her daughter there after completing her work at the municipal offices. Everyone had assumed Kiernan was at a friend's. There was no note, but there seldom was. At eight o'clock, they tried him on his cell phone. Calling from the kitchen, they didn't hear the phone ring in Kiernan's pocket upstairs. After all, the house was designed to muffle sound with its plush carpets and oak doors between the kitchen and family room.

Of course, they checked with the housekeeper, but she hadn't seen the boy the entire day. She'd assumed he'd gotten up and gone out without eating breakfast.

By ten o'clock, Kiernan's mother asked her husband to come down from his office, and together, they began to phone Kiernan's friends, at least the ones they knew. They sent Linda to bed. She was old enough to wander upstairs and get herself sorted out. She was in her bathroom, which backed on to Kiernan's, when her parents phoned their son again. That's when Kiernan's sister heard her brother's ringtone on the other side of the wall. It was a sample of Nickelback he'd downloaded. He'd shown his father, she remembered. Her father had thought it was funny but told Kiernan not to download too many ringtones, because they were expensive.

"Mom," Linda shouted as she came out of her bedroom and walked into Kiernan's, "I can hear his phone up here." She walked through his room, which was tidied each day by the housekeeper. No dirty clothes or boy smell amid rotting heaps of soggy gym gear. Just a made bed and a fish tank kept clean and algae-free by a company hired to keep it that way. Linda could still hear the phone ringing as she knocked on the bathroom door. Then she pushed it open to find her brother lying between the bathtub and the toilet. The curtain at the window was open, she remembers. Why is he sleeping there? she wondered, until she saw the blood and the knife and screamed.

A few days later, Kiernan was discharged from the hospital after he and his parents promised to attend family counseling. Though Kiernan had passed out, he actually hadn't done as much damage as he might have. His passing out might have been due as much to the shock of seeing his own blood pooling at his feet as to the harm he'd done. It didn't really matter. Something would now have to change.

The Connecting Places

No size of house is necessarily right or wrong; no suburb intrinsically bad or good. It's what we do with the spaces in which we live: To build a mansion and forget that a small family will live inside its expansive space is to forget our responsibility to our kids.

Our connections with one another are profoundly shaped by the physical spaces we occupy. Human geographers, urban planners, architects, sociologists, and ecologists have developed an impressive library of studies showing that physical space affects mental well-being, relationship patterns, even physical health and longevity.[1] Unfortunately, few suburbs are planned with those studies in mind. Instead, we have forgotten all about organic cities that grow naturally over time, preferring planned patterns of habitation that leave us fulfilled as consumers but despondent as citizens.

Raising a We Generation is easier in some spaces than others. Kiernan is alone amid riches. Like a fairy-tale prince in a palace, he has wants that lie beyond his fortress walls: everyday connections with others. His life lacks the struggle and turmoil that make for communities and the genuineness of touch and responsibility for others.

If there is a threat to the We Generation, it is the cloistering of children inside the large homes of the middle class, the structures' very spaciousness breaking down family interactions, programming all interaction, denying the informality that allows us to offer ourselves to each other spontaneously. There are fewer and fewer family hearths around which to huddle and pass stories from one generation to the next.

Our children are feeling abandoned amid material abundance.

I worry something is wrong in those large suburban homes. We create the illusion of what we want, but miss the substance. Selling a home, vendors are told to bake cookies before they hold an open house. To turn on all the lights to make the place look cheerful. To declutter, to make the spaces open, inviting.

It's a superficial solution that blinds us to what our children need: connections, a family space, with parents and children cluttering each other's lives.

In the United States, the average home has grown from 983 square feet in 1950 to 2,434 square feet in 2005. It's a trend seen across the Western world. That footprint is coming at a price, and not just environmentally. I think it is more than coincidence that over that same period, North American scores on an international survey of happiness have dropped and the amount of time we spend with our children has decreased. There is simply little or no benefit to buying bigger houses if doing so threatens our relationships with our children, our neighbors, and our spouses.

Besides, it takes a lot of extra hours at work to afford the minimansion and the two cars that are required to sustain a family in the suburbs. If we calculate the actual cost of owning a second vehicle, it averages out to between five and seven thousand dollars a year. That's after-tax dollars. Assuming even a modest tax rate of 35 percent, owning that second car means having to earn between seven and ten thousand dollars a year in extra salary. If one is earning in the range of $80,000 a year, it would take an entire month to pay for the second car, something that could be avoided by living closer to one's workplace or in a community with denser housing.

It doesn't take long to see that we are working for nothing except empty spaces at home and long commutes back and forth from houses too big to connect with our families in. It's not something the average suburban parent wants to consider. We get attached to our gleaming kitchens, tidy gardens, and detached lifestyles. We think of denser housing developments as less safe.

But I'm not so sure.

When I ask kids where they'd like to live, they tell me they'd rather live where they can navigate their own way to the store, school, and friends. They rarely mention square footage. Most children would be happy to give up large rooms and en suite bathrooms for a greater amount of personal freedom, a cohesive community, and time with parents who are less stressed.

A Less-than-Radiant City

A National Film Board of Canada release called *Radiant City* is a stark, sarcastic attempt by filmmaker Gary Burns and journalist Jim Brown to tell the story of the suburbs from the perspective of one family. Splicing the very individual decisions of suburban migrants with expert testimony, *Radiant City* gives us an anthropologist's insight into *Homo suburbanitus*. It is as bleak a picture as found in the Academy Award–winning film *American Beauty*. Both portray a grayness that contrasts with the perky advertisements in newspapers for family homes beyond the city gridlock.

The strange thing is that what we want in our suburbs is exactly what we have downtown. If we think about it, what we want is the urban community, in which work, recreation, shopping, and our house are all seamlessly connected. We want to feel as though our children's school is as much a part of our community as our homes and offices. We want that warm, fuzzy feeling we get when we pass old men playing bocce together on close-cropped grass, and children riding tricycles around fountains while we walk to catch a bus to work. We want to nod to our neighbors. We want to walk to a great Mexican tapas restaurant nestled beside a coffee shop and an English pub. We want that integrated community of our childhoods, whether real or imagined in celluloid.

It can't be found in the suburbs. It can't be found inside monstrous homes. It is exactly what our children need, though. In its absence, they have had to find a sense of We on the computer, in chat rooms, and through virtual gaming. If we lament how our children connect, and miss them being close, we have only ourselves to blame for the structures we have provided them.

The New Urbanism

The worst cities I've encountered are ones without a living center. Few people live there. There are no shops. No grocery stores. No nightlife. Just empty towers after five o'clock. There are solutions, however. A new urbanism is growing inside our cities. The new urbanism sews us back together. Higher-density dwellings are designed with the single-car garage pointed into a back alley. There are porches out front. When units are stacked three and four high, there are places to look down onto the street.

It's a case of everything old is new again.

I grew up in Montreal's suburbs, but reversed the migration and moved downtown, back to the same streets where my father grew up. He lived three doors down from Mordecai Richler, the author and social commentator. His boyhood neighborhood is picturesque in its streetscape. Flats rise two and three high above the sidewalk. Wrought-iron stairways coil their way up to each front door. People keep tidy, postage-stamp-size gardens that are the responsibility of the first-floor owners. The streets are alive with trees and children. If kids want to play, they use the parks that are positioned every few blocks. There are recreation centers nearby with open gyms. A wonderful shopping district lets you buy imported cheese from New Zealand and Greek wine. There is a bagel factory that bakes its doughy, handmade twists in wood-fired ovens all night long. After an evening of theater a short bus ride away, you can buy a dozen of these treats, along with cream cheese and smoked salmon. On warm summer nights, you sit on the front steps or back balconies and listen for the sounds of the evening: a child's cry; a couple arguing; teenagers talking as they walk by holding hands; old people, if they are still up, trading stories and smoking.

Our suburban homes put all these layers of life in one small venue. We socialize, entertain, and recreate, even work, inside those hermetically sealed boxes. Enjoy a game of pool? Build a billiards room in the basement. Want to talk? Go online. Need to work? Commandeer a bedroom and create a home office. Need food? Enjoy the palatial kitchen, bigger than the one in the small, family-run Mexican takeout I used to frequent on rue Mont Royal.

All this order actually threatens our children's sovereignty. They can no longer play with other children safely, because the sight lines have been broken. They need us to drive them everywhere and pay for activities. They need technology to find one another after school. They need to consume, because that is all they really are now: purchasers. Their role is to keep filling up the boxes.

I see children lost amid the wealth and security we've squandered. The Kiernans of our community are being suffocated. What they want is something far different from the world we've provided, in which each family drives alone, plays alone, exercises alone. Is alone.

Quite remarkable, really, that our children are still reaching out and creating community at all. They are a generation searching for connections in ways far different from generations before them. Those connections can look very different. In what was once a quiet country town, there is now a growing "bedroom community" an hour and a half north of

Toronto. Children as young as ten are left at home alone weekday mornings before school so their parents can commute the congested highways to office buildings that ring the city. A strange and unexpected thing has been happening in the schools. There is now a breakfast program. It's not there to feed children hungry for food, but to provide the kids with a safe and caring atmosphere in which to break bread. It has been remarkably successful. The children walk or are bused and then share time with adult volunteers. There is a small fee, and parents willingly pay to know that their kids are looked after.

Where there are no breakfast clubs, there are kids' help lines. I hear from the volunteers that most of their calls are from lonely kids looking for contact with an adult, someone to hear them talk about their lives. Not all those kids are from the suburbs, but I know from my clinical practice that there are more than we would expect.

It's sad, but hopeful at the same time. At least the kids are still reaching out.

The Right-Sized House and a Solid Connection to One's Community

By itself, a large dysfunctional house needn't sound the death knell for a sense of belonging to a family and home. However, the lifestyle of economically advantaged families can compound the obstacles these homes pose to nurturing a We Generation. Parents working long hours at workplaces that require long commutes and living in big houses in anonymous suburbs may unintentionally put their children at risk.

If you're worried about this pattern, ask yourself the following questions:

1. Do I use all the space in my home?
   • Consider: If your house is so large that you don't bump into your kids often, then that means your kids can't find you, either.
2. Do I have enough time for my family? If I live in the suburbs and commute, what price do I pay in regard to the quality of my family life? If I live in the countryside, what benefits does that bring? If I'm in the city, how do I take advantage of the shorter commute?
   • Consider: If the location of your house requires you to drive or use public transit to and from work, and you are traveling a great distance, then you probably have less time to connect with your children. Are there other solutions to finding a balanced quality of life and economic security?
3. How much time each day do I spend with my children?
   • Consider: If you're not at home very much, how will you influence your children's psychological and social development?
4. How much do I work?
   • Consider: Several TV sets, a backyard pool, and other unnecessary gadgets and playthings may be fun, but are your children getting what they need most: your attention? Would fewer gadgets and more time be more meaningful to the kids?
5. How much time do I have to contribute to my community?
   • Consider: If your work is all-consuming, how do you find time to model for your children We-thinking behavior toward your neighbors and friends?

Solutions to Fragile Connections

No one single factor necessarily puts children like Kiernan at risk. But add them all up, and suddenly, our connections become fragile. A houseful of diversions such as televisions and computers suddenly lurks ominously, threatening our children's well-being. Make those suburban mansions self-sufficient, self-cleaning, and hived off from neighbors, and we also take away opportunities for our children to contribute to the welfare of others: to cook, clean, look after elderly grandparents, or do a good deed for a neighbor.

A family I know has worried its way through these problems. Like thousands of others, this family enjoys its 2,856-square-foot home with the walkout basement and small backyard garden, two-car garage, gleaming kitchen, walk-in closets, and main-floor laundry room. But they also realize the risk the suburb poses. The parents, Matt and Wendy, have done what they can, by taking different risks. Matt has started his own business. It means longer hours, but gives him the flexibility to work at home. He's not tied to the office routine. He can pick his children up from the private school they attend, where values are more important than end-of-term, standardized exams. Its classes are kept to a manageable size.

At home, Matt and Wendy make sure they know their neighbors. Last summer, they closed the block and had a wonderful street party. The activity has changed how people relate to one another across fences. People now shout hello, drop by to borrow tools or maybe a few eggs when a splurge of baking on Sunday afternoon leaves them short.

Wendy has decided to cut back to half-time on her work hours, too. She's a flight attendant and can job share. It will mean a little less seniority and will decrease her pension, but lately, she's been feeling that all the time away from her two boys is leaving her empty.

Everyone in the family compromises to make these new changes work. There's still the basics, but now the cars the family owns are used rather than new. The kids don't do expensive activities, but are getting a good education. Weekends are time for church and connecting with extended family, who live an hour's drive away.

Doing Chores

Matt and Wendy's solutions are removing the threat their suburban home poses. There are lots of possible strategies besides the route they chose. Take chores, for example, which can help promote a healthy generation of considerate kids. Who, after all, is cleaning those monster homes? If not the children, then what message are they learning about responsibility for themselves and others?

Miriam Kaufman, a pediatrician at Toronto's Hospital for Sick Children, says, "In my practice, I see so many families where the child is such a precious little darling you would never dream of telling him or her to clean up around the house."[2] It comes as no surprise, then, that Marilyn Rossman, a professor of family education who led a twenty-year study of parents and children, showed that the most reliable gauge of how likely kids are to turn out well was whether or not they did chores growing up.

That's the strange thing about providing our children with too much. They lose the advantages of having to take responsibility. They are at risk of never developing a sense of themselves as competent, caring contributors to their communities or families.

Repair the Plumbing

A house is an organic structure. I've built a few from scratch. It's an intricate exercise in matching all the parts. Walls are roughed in before the plumbing is laid and the electrical wiring installed. You always have to be thinking of the last step, which will seal the interconnected services behind walls of gypsum and wood.

But what about the family that will live there? Do we stop to consider how we will connect within those walls? How we will naturally bump into each other? How we will make our children feel a part of their family? Nurturing a sense of responsibility for ourselves and others is as much about how we structure our children's lives as what we ask them to do. The physicality of their lives opens and closes opportunities to think We.

How many of us would say we were really worse off for having shared a room with a sibling? How many of us would say that the size of our rooms really mattered while we were growing up? Or was it the control we had and the attachments we felt when at home with our parents that made a difference in our lives?

Parents have shown me lots of ways to ensure that their houses help each member feel a part of the family:

- *Put the children's play area close to the kitchen.* The kitchen is the hub. If we want to make our children feel that we're close by, we need to create a comfortable space for them where they can be seen.
- *Put the computer in a place in the house where parents naturally pass by.* Your children will be safer, won't need "netnanny" software to keep an eye on them, and can still listen in to the rest of the household, even if they are zoned out with their headphones on.
- *Have one family room where there is one television.* When it comes to family spaces, fewer is better. If our goal is to raise a We Generation, then learning compromise when it comes to sharing the remote control offers an opportunity for life-long social skills.

- *Integrate family functions.* Make spaces multipurpose so that play areas are close to work areas, entertainment nestles close to where people want to sit and relax. The more spaces work together, the more likely people are to position themselves side by side. It will be a little noisy at times, but then how many hours a day do we have with our kids, anyway?
- *Have a family pet that everyone has responsibility to look after.* An animal in the house, or outside, makes family members interact. A dog, cat, guinea pig, or rabbit, or even a horse, has to be fed and cared for. Our houses have to have spaces inside and out to allow us to tend to the animal's needs. It is a group project that teaches responsibility.
- *Give children chores so that they feel ownership for their space.* They shouldn't just be cleaning their own rooms; they should be cleaning the common spaces, too. In the process, they learn they have something important to give back to others.
- *Have a creative area, a workshop or garage, where projects in progress don't have to be put away each day.* A project space also means an opportunity for one-on-one time together as a parent and child work through a problem: a school science experiment, building a shelf for a bedroom, fixing the lawnmower, or knocking together a go-cart.
- *If there are family members with a passion for music, position the instruments where they can be heard throughout the house.* Music should be shared. Children need to feel they are noticed and applauded. They also need to learn when to compromise and wait to practice.

- *Build a porch*. Put a swing on it so there is a place to sit when the weather is good. Kids love hammocks. There is something about rocking and sunlight that brings out the best in us.
- *Let your kids destroy your lawn with lots of little feet and water fights and bicycles*. Lawns should be used. Grass can be replanted. Lawns can be spaces where children play and adults garden nearby. Keeping everything too pristine only sends our children away from us. There will be lots of time in our old age for perfect gardens.

If some of these ideas sound positively wacky, even heretical, it's because we've made our homes into isolated zones rather than organic spaces for connections. We put the music room far from the television. We let children play in the basement so that we can listen to music alone in the kitchen. We insist everyone have his or her own work space. Dad is in the garage. Mom is in her craft room. The children each do their own thing apart from one another.

Our children grow up alone.

The zeitgeist of the new family is leaving us confused. In the space of just a few generations, we've leaped from the agrarian family, in which all family functions were integrated in a single-room house, to homes that ramble and divide. What we can afford to build, we do, whether we need to build it or not. We don't want to think about the consequences until it's too late and our sons and daughters are pushing us aside as easily as we let them disappear from our lives.

If we are lonely for our children's attention, look first at the brick-and-mortar worlds in which we have raised them. If we are anxious about our children's thinking Me instead of We, critically examine the structures in which we've housed them.

We Need *Communitas*

At the same time that our homes are becoming empty of connectivity, social organizations are realizing that tightly woven relationships keep young people attached. Take universities. Declining enrollments forecasted for the future have made university administrators painfully aware that more than a third of all students who enter their first year leave without completing their degree. That's a lot of money leaving campuses. As universities give more thought to their bottom lines, they have been realizing that they need better retention schemes.

Carleton University in Ottawa, with a sprawling suburban campus of 23,000 students, has created the ArtsOne program. As the brochure explains, "When you enroll in ArtsOne, you join a community of 100 first-year students who share a common timetable, instructors, reading material, and classrooms for four of your courses. In ArtsOne, you have the opportunity to make connections—connections between the courses you are taking and connections with other students learning the same things you are learning." First-year students volunteer to participate. It's a clever strategy to challenge the anonymity of large lecture halls.

If Carleton's experiment works, it is because it provides more than just the idea of community. It places young people in close quarters with others who need them and are needed. Victor Turner has called small, intentional gatherings such as this *communitas*.[3] Small congregations that come together for rituals related to healing and learning help to sustain us in ways larger groups cannot. Eye contact, sitting next to the same person week after week, the assurance of sustained proximity, combine to make education a more personal affair.

Those same themes are as important in our homes as they are in our institutions.

Give our young people an opportunity to connect, and they will. They will cluster into networks with those with whom they find a kinship of values. They will look for others who mirror back to them something special about themselves. It is as if, over time, in our communitas, we find others who are our match. Our children are likely to experience an odd sense of validation when they meet their doppelgängers, others who reflect back their own interests and passions. Out there, amid millions of others, there are people who share something with us. Doppelgängers who mirror not our looks, but our thoughts and dreams.

Intentional Communities

Our children have as much need as adults do to reach out to one another. One way to meet this need is an *intentional community*. Though still relatively rare, these communities are growing in number. Middle-aged, middle-class individuals and families are banding together in blocks of townhouses and apartments with a twist. To these individual living units have been added communal kitchens, shared automobiles, community gardens, common rooms for television, exercise, and meetings, subcommittees for social activism and recreation, and, of course, a collective sense of responsibility for one another. Where once these were the domain of hippies, whose group politics and lack of business acumen left many collectives as dysfunctional as suburban blocks, today they are more sophisticated. We find these intentional communities even in upscale neighborhoods. Members buy a part of the community's real estate. Their share, like the value of the property it-self, increases as market prices rise.

The model is relatively simple, with more than one hundred cohousing projects successfully developed in the United States. Most include some variation of two- and three-bedroom townhouses and smaller apartments clustered around a common house and courtyard that contain a large kitchen and dining area, a lounge, a playroom, a laundry, a TV room, guest accommodations, and a workshop. The arrangements can offer residents a small-town feeling inside the city. Originating in Denmark three decades ago, the cohousing concept creates an intergenerational community with lots of opportunities to interact. Common meals, work groups, and monthly governance meetings provide residents with a chance to connect with one another and to have a say in creating a sustainable, environmentally friendly living space.

Cohousing and similar efforts are addressing the risks posed to a generation of children from small families. The shrinking size of most families, coupled with larger and larger homes, means that our children are being raised without having to share. University dorm builders know this; it's rare now for new dorms to be built with shared accommodation. Instead, each student is given a small room to himself or herself. It's easier that way. Our kids expect to be by themselves.

It's at this level of the practical and structural that we see the tipping point for our children. They may value connections, but those monster homes are raising a selfish generation that does not understand the concept We. It's a complex problem that is only aggravated when we keep making our living spaces larger.

Turning Houses into Homes

Though some forms of housing may offer more hope for a We Generation to grow, at the end of the day it's not the house that makes the difference, but how well one's house is made a home. That means ensuring that our families work at least as well as does the plumbing and electrical systems of any residence we build or occupy.

This is particularly important to consider when modifying where we live by building, renovating, or moving. Our motivation to change the shape of our physical space can range from the dysfunctional (thinking bigger is better, showing off to the neighbors, greed) to the compassionate (the kids need a little more space, an elderly parent needs to move in with us, a more environmentally sound house will save energy). Many families, though, have arrived at my office on the verge of breaking up at the very moment when their new house is ready to be occupied. Often, the problem is that my clients have done everything they could to ensure their family's material well-being, but ignored the relationships that bind family members together.

It's understandable. Amid the difficult work of creating something from nothing, we can too easily lose focus.

That loss of focus explains a lot about what happened to Frank and Vivian after Frank discovered a derelict cottage that had been languishing on a hill overlooking the village where his family had raised him.[4] Abandoned by its owner, the structure was surrounded by weed-choked gardens that hid the stone barn that had been sinking into the mossy ground for more than a century. Here and there were bits of color from the rose bushes and lilac trees that now grew wild. The house's two-foot-thick stone walls still stood solid, though. Not so fortunate were the plaster walls inside. They had mildewed as roof joists corrupted with rot and age had made the roof, or what was left of it, a sagging, dangerous undulation.

Frank thought the place was perfect, and Vivian agreed when she saw it a week later, though she remembered feeling an overwhelming flood of anxiety that something about this house would demand more of her than she was ready to give. She had brushed that feeling aside. It was, after all, an inexpensive property with loads of potential. Their two children, aged seven and four, would love it, once it was done.

They both reasoned that if Frank took on the project and Vivian picked up most of Frank's responsibilities around the house, they could create a beautiful home in just one year, and the mortgage they'd take on would still be manageable. With a small bungalow thirty kilometers away, it would mean compromises, as Frank would be away from the family while the renovations were being done. But they were both up for a little inconvenience. The extent of that inconvenience, neither she nor Frank could foresee.

Soon Frank found himself occupied most days after work and on weekends. As the project took over the family's life, Vivian was forced to do more child-care. She'd joke with her friends, when she had time to see them, that she was a single parent in all but name. The joke lost its humor when Frank was home late for the tenth time and the children went to bed without a story from their dad.

As a three-time home builder myself, I am saddened to encounter so many couples whose marriages become as derelict as that cottage because of their best efforts to build a new home for themselves and their children. Ironically, as the new building emerges sturdy and sound, the family's relationship cracks and buckles under the strain of the project. It is as if those responsible for building have neglected to maintain the structure that already exists, the family that is to live in the home they are passionately constructing.

In Frank and Vivian's case, their relationship ended and the new house was sold. Vivian moved to a bungalow near where she and the kids used to live. Frank was just happy to be done with the place. He wonders now if the place was what he had really wanted. Besides, both he and Vivian said the quarrels, stress, and misspent time made the new place seem, in the end, far less attractive than it had looked in their dreams. Selling it brought closure to a difficult period in both their lives.

Strategies to Build Houses That Are Homes

A family that has children and that is making such a major life transition may want to consider several things when undertaking the building of a new home, a major renovation, or a move. If what the members of the family want at the end is a home, and not just a house, they will need to keep an eye out for threats to the very relationships they want their new home to celebrate. Here are a few pointers from families who've survived the ordeal still connected to each other.

1. *Fair is fair.* How much time is the person leading the project going to be given to do the work? In his or her absence, there is still child-care and the maintenance of existing properties to be managed, and income to be earned. Usually, the one most passionate about the project leads the building or renovating, but seeing someone enjoying his or her sweat equity as much as most home builders do can leave the less involved spouse and children angry and re-

sentful. Who is the new house for? The individual builder or the entire family?

2. *Timing is everything.* Even if a family can agree that one person will take on the project, families need to look at whether this is the right time to build, renovate, or move. For example, it's often those on limited incomes, early in their marriages, or starting families who build from scratch so that they can get the enjoyment from their new homes sooner than later. There is usually a powerful vision of how things will be after the house is built, and a naive disregard for all the magic that is being missed when long weekends get consumed with laying a foundation, putting on siding, or painting empty rooms. We already know the dangers of over-work at the office. Our passion to build the house we've always wanted can be equally blinding.

3. *Set a pace that suits the whole family.* Most young builders and renovators react to the problem of timing by trying to work faster. "Short-term pain for long-term gain" is the most common reasoning. It can be a slippery slope, depending on just how much time the project consumes. Summer cottages often bring with them this very problem. A long summer's work might get the job done and result in a livable home ready for the next season. But too often, the next summer is a flurry of activity, finishing decks, docks, and landscaping. What was to be a single summer's work can quickly become two or three summers of hectic activity. Better, I say, to simply accept that home renovation takes time and agree to a three-year project. This, of course, can be tricky if bank financing is involved, as the bank will insist on a quicker construction to protect its investment. One might have to hire people to help, if the goal is to have the family intact when the family cottage is ready.

4. *Get everyone involved.* I've noticed that families that are torn apart by a construction project or getting a new home ready tend to have made the project one person's responsibility. The less involved spouse and, occasionally, the kids walk through floor plans or comment on the placement of stud walls and the color of paint for the bedrooms, but the art of building or renovating is seldom shared. A preferred plan is for the more involved member of the family to play the role of general contractor and get other family members as involved as time allows. Less involved spouses need to be freed up to shop for fixtures and new windows, do the budget, or arrange landscaping. These are all big jobs for anyone self-contracting, and they demand time. This will probably mean the person knocking nails will have to agree to leave the job site to prepare meals, clean bathrooms, and transport children to after-school activities. In the process, the kids will be watching and learning.

5. *Even children have a role to play in the construction or renovation of a house.* Kids love to plan decks and treehouses. They can help to tidy up the job site. The more it's their house, the less grumbling one will hear back home when children pick up extra chores that used to be done by the parent who is away at the construction site. A child who sees her contribution giving Mom and Dad time to frame up a special loft in her new room is likely to become just as excited as the adults about the building project and future move.

6. *Finally, document the history of the family's new home.* Make sure that photos and videos show the progress made and each person's contribution. This record becomes a story about how the family grew closer as the structure they were building went up.

In my professional practice, I see competent home builders and renovators struggle with these six issues with their families. Normal stressors like the birth of children, an aging parent, the unexpected onset of an illness, even moving into the new home, add greatly to the stress of getting one's house built right. Being a home builder is difficult enough. Recognizing that it takes place while life is dishing up one unexpected crisis after another can save a parent from losing focus regarding what a new house is really about.

When it comes to raising a We Generation, it's important to remember that our children are watching not just what we do but also how we do it. A parent who becomes obsessed with the material world and begins missing the important events in a child's life teaches the children that relationships come second. It's the same for the child who is watching two parents muddle through negotiations over what is and is not an equitable distribution of work. Relationships can quickly become battlegrounds where the definition of "fair contribution" is entangled in the politics of gender, status, and pride.

Pepper Schwartz, an American sociologist, speaks of peer marriage as one in which both partners are valued for the contribution they make.[5] It's a good model to show our children. Contribution can be measured in many ways, not just monetarily or by who hammers the most nails. In this time of a heightened sense of gender politics, old wounds can be opened when the one doing the construction (usually Dad) leaves the other spouse (usually Mom) looking after the children, elderly parents, or perhaps alone to keep the old house going while the new one is raised.

Many couples are surprised by how much the negative experience of building comes to overshadow their anticipated joy of owning a new home. Many children say they wished their family had just stayed put. Where we adults see the need for bigger bedrooms and multiple bathrooms, I find most children just want to be close with those they love and experience a calm household in which to grow.

Successful Family Home Builders

Henri and Geneviève managed to navigate these minefields. They built a modest home that sits on a high, dry piece of land with fifty acres of mixed forest behind them. By most standards, the house is not opulent, despite its use of passive solar technologies. It is a tidy, functional place where window seats are well placed to take advantage of the sun during quiet spring afternoons. During the building, Henri took the lead most of the time, but he was careful to involve Geneviève in the process. Though she wasn't comfortable enough with construction to, say, get up on the roof and shingle it, Geneviève became handy with a saw and hammer. The two balanced the need to work on the home with the care of their nine-month-old. They asked friends and extended family to help, not only with the building, but also by providing childcare so that Geneviève could be on site as much as possible. Henri also took a leave from his work for six weeks each summer for two years. The couple reasoned that they would do better financially putting his sweat equity into the house than buying services with after-tax dollars. They finished with a house that was ready six months before the birth of their second child.

Good stories like this offer clues for success. They speak to the capacity of families to strengthen relationships as they build their dream homes. Too often the stories are more like those of Wanda and Peter, who completed a fifty-thousand-dollar addition to their home that included an outdoor hot tub and screened deck. A middle-aged man with three teenagers, Peter couldn't understand his wife's and children's anger at his working overtime to pay for the project or their resentment when he spent time with the contractor ensuring every detail was perfect. Peter had thought his family wanted the addition. What he didn't understand was that Wanda and the kids needed Peter's attention even more.

Building a home, after all, is as much about building the family that is to live there as it is about laying the foundation for a sturdy structure.

Healthier Home Lives

When faced with change, families need what psychologists Hamilton McCubbin and Laurie McCubbin (they are father and daughter) have described as the ability to adjust and adapt.[6] The ability to adjust means one's family is able and has the resources to maintain its integrity when under assault. There must be enough emotional support, attachments between family members must be strong, and extended family, neighbors, and friends must be available when needed. Think of the crisis that follows the death of a child, and one quickly appreciates just how important it is to have resources. In dealing with interrupted work schedules, emotional tears, and the logistics of funerals, families with lots of resources adjust more quickly than those who are isolated.

Sometimes, though, a family's resources are depleted: The family's principal breadwinner becomes ill; the family may have recently moved to a new community; there is no extended family or close friends to rely upon in a crisis. In those cases, families have to adapt rather than adjust. New patterns of interaction are needed. New resources need culti-vating. Transformation becomes the goal if stress is to be kept in check.

Many people prefer to turn to other family members when help is needed. But what happens when there is no ex-tended family nearby, or when one would rather not ask family for assistance? Maybe the congregation at the family's place of worship is willing to act as a sort of surrogate fam-ily and offer support. Neighbors, too, may be willing to help if they perceive this as an opportunity to make their contri-bution to their community.

Family crises come in many forms. We model for our chil-dren good problem solving when we look for ways to adapt that sew us into the fabric of our families and communities. For example, if your family has relied on one parent to be the breadwinner and suddenly circumstances change, the econ-omy tanks, and it's the other parent who has to work outside the home, then new patterns of interaction and dependency are going to be needed. When that happens, a family must as-sess its resources. Are there grandparents or neighbors who can lend a hand now and again when both parents have to be at work? Are there ways to carpool children to activities, or share cooking responsibilities with friends who have children the same age? Every time the day-to-day workings of a fam-ily get modified, new solutions need to be found and new rules for how things get done must be negotiated. Different families will handle these transformations in different ways. A very private family may have to realize it's okay to get help from others. A family where there has traditionally been just one breadwinner may have to adjust to both spouses working outside the home.

Closer and More Personal Spaces

A We Generation needs its parents up close and personal. It needs to weather good times and bad. It doesn't necessarily need excessive material support and bigger bathrooms. In fact, there is little to suggest that living in a wealthier neighborhood or a bigger home is associated with better-behaved kids or happier families.

The truth is that those middle-class suburbs have as high an incidence of, say, teenage drug use as do poorer communities. Middle-class children are still potential victims of abuse. Children still commit suicide, die in car accidents, and run away. Even middle-class kids in pristine burbs have problems, many of which are actually related to where they live. As American psychologist Suniya Luthar noted in her studies, affluent youth report significantly higher levels of anxiety and greater depression than less-well-off children. They also smoke and abuse drugs and alcohol more than inner-city students.[7]

If we are leaving the inner city for utopia, we might be forgetting that suburbs often don't suit children, especially teenagers, very well at all. They are a wasteland when it comes to opportunities for kids to think We. Instead, excessive dependency on parents for drives and few places to hang out beyond their basements can create anxiety and provoke patterns of self-medication to cope with the overwhelming feelings of disconnection. Rural settings may be a better choice, when they are accessible. At least there children can find opportunities for adventure and sometimes even tightly knit communities that are willing to integrate them.

So how do the kids cope when they feel like outsiders or are cast into the role of mindless consumers? Unfortunately, by embracing their status as "other." Nick Barham spent a year encountering the Technicolor variety of young people across Britain. He documents in *Disconnected* a generation of hedonistic, drug-abusing, freewheeling, youth whom the media have vilified.[8] There is reason to be concerned, but also reason to celebrate a generation that is resisting conformity.

Beneath the mayhem, Barham finds something hopeful, something similar to what I've witnessed in my clinical work with teens over the past twenty years. As Barham tells us, after his year-long sojourn amid the kids:

> The strategies of disconnection—from the past, from mainstream politics, from traditional forms of education, from taboos and shame, from duty, and more importantly from reality—are not those of a stupid uncaring, vacuous bunch. They are practical, sociable and often enjoyable responses to a world that is difficult for everyone, and within which a new code of existence is still being created. Rather than finding this degree of disconnection discouraging or upsetting . . . my impression is British youth had become more positive. I felt cheered by my contact with boy racers, with drug users and graffiti artists. Within these frowned-on activities I had found beauty and humor. Friendliness and energy. The kind of things that make living worthwhile.[9]

It's a positive portrayal of the chaos, a sensitive portrayal of a generation that is not as morally ambiguous as we might think, nor as destructive as our media portray them to be. In the end, Barham finds the kids actually quite conservative, seeking standards, making judgments. And yet, their moral compass can appear on the surface so different from their parents'. They don't look like their parents or act like them in their daily regimes. Hence the conflict and our moral panic about youth today.

Can we blame the kids? What have we left them with to create an identity in the barrens we call our communities? I prefer to see the passion of youth manifest in exuberance rather than in the dropout culture of two decades ago, when kids seemed to have given up. Said they couldn't give a f—— about anyone or anything. That was my generation's blight.

Barham tells us, "We should be proud of our disconnected generation."[10] While they may be disconnecting from the monochrome values of their parents, who have bought into illusions of consumption-derived happiness, these young people are trying to remain connected in ways that we never imagined when we were their age. Kicking back at social norms may be middle-class children's best solution to emotional neglect. They disconnect from social norms while connecting to a peer group that values one another. That's the We Generation's way.

Keep Focused

The solution isn't necessarily to sell everything and move into an 800-square-foot mobile home or live in the cramped confines of a decaying inner-city townhouse. It is, however, to stay focused on what families need, whether in big houses or small, downtown or the suburbs, a farm or a village:

- *Think about what you're losing.* Step back and ask some difficult questions about how one's living space affects family members' connections. Is working harder to afford bigger the best use of time and money? What is really gained from building, renovating, or moving?

What are the real costs in terms of quality time with family, friends, and community? What price, emotionally and financially, are family members willing to pay?

- *Bigger can be better, sometimes.* Of course, there are times when it can make sense to go big. A family with lots of guests needs a guest room. Gardeners might appreciate a bigger deck with a view of their flower beds. Our homes are, after all, part of our self-expression. But we still need to ask ourselves before we uproot the kids, Will we be mortgaged to the point we have no life? Will our family find the things it most wants: healthy relationships, time to entertain and look at the garden, and less stress?

- *Location, location, location.* We choose our house by balancing what we can afford with the kind of community we want. However, cheaper square footage can bring with it longer commutes, longer periods of childcare, and the added expense of keeping two cars running. It's not that the price we pay isn't necessarily worth it. Many families, however, never look closely at what they are giving up before they sign the mortgage papers.

- *Competing dreams.* A couple may want the same house, but not the same lifestyle in the house. Families often find they get into conflict over how to use their space: Should the spare room be a children's playroom, a music room, a place for the television, or a sewing and craft space? Should there be a big garden or a picture-perfect lawn? Are there places where kids can make a mess, or is their mess going to be tolerated everywhere? Should the house be used as a bed and breakfast, or rooms rented to students? There can be many visions for one space.

New Families, Old Patterns

Let's face it, what we really want is the mythical community we imagine existed a half century ago. We breathe lustily at the thought of a community of connected parts. A paperboy riding his bike down a clean sidewalk launching papers over hedgerows. Pretty dogs being walked by adults who stop and chat while children run through lawn sprinklers. We imagine a community where thinking We is easy for kids.

I'm not sure many of us are going to find that ideal.

The strange paradox is that the more people strive for extrinsic goals like flashy clothes and the latest cell phone, the more their problems multiply. "I am what I buy" is a surefire formula for unhappiness. It's a dirty little secret parents don't like to admit, especially when it comes to our kids. After all, if all our striving for bigger and better homes, in safer and prettier suburbs, isn't really helping to raise children who will become loving citizens, then what exactly is the point?

Tips List

Surviving life in the suburbs, or in the city, means new solutions for new times. Here's some of the better advice I've heard from parents who are trying to teach their kids to be part of a weave of relationships:

- Put your kids in day-care at least half a day a week. Even my dog needs to be socialized. Our children, too, need to encounter rooms full of other children.
- Downsize your house. Avoid the clutter that big closets and basements breed. Buy one of each item you need, and teach kids to share.

- Live close to your work. Save the planet, save time, save money, and make life at home a whole lot less stressful.
- Rent if you have to in order to live in a community where there is a better quality of connections. The money you spend won't be wasted.
- Remind your children of their roots. If you can, visit or live close to a place where your family feels connected.
- Model for your children how to be a part of their family and community. Be sure they see you volunteering, networking, and doing random acts of kindness.
- Make your home a place from which people come and go. Encourage people to drop in. Worry less if the house is tidy and more about whether people feel comfortable visiting on a whim.

chapter **eight**

Village People

There is a story older than the Bible of a king who tells his people that he has placed his child among them, but does not tell them which child is his. The king says he will reward all those who are kind to the child after the youngster has grown. Predictably, all the children in the kingdom are treated well, as everyone seeks to curry favor and fortune from the king. It is a parable that children's rights activists have used to support their argument for the UN Convention on the Rights of the Child and other similar global efforts to eradicate child poverty, land mines (which kill and maim far more children than they injure combatants), child laborers, and the sexual exploitation and trafficking of children.

All children are our children. All children benefit from being supported by a community of concern. All seek, in one way or another, to hear from their communities:

- "You belong."
- "You're trustworthy."

- "You're capable."
- "You're responsible."

Those are the foundational messages a We Generation needs to hear, not just from parents but from every quarter of the community. Within the collective commons, it is our role as parents and elders to provide opportunities for these messages to be heard by every child.

I'm not sure we are doing our job very well. Judging by the number of youth who are still disconnected, we've got to do more to nurture a We Generation. Zygmunt Bauman, a sociologist, sees our communities disintegrating under the weight of personal freedoms.[1] We no longer commit to our communities. We wear our identity as a member lightly, a cloak we easily shed when something better comes along. According to Bauman, we only ever join together when some spectacle is there to engage us. An election. A fire. A child abduction. At such times, we become a community, blending our individual interests with the interests of others.

Community, though, cannot be built on such superficiality. Alienated individuals, like iPod-listening kids on the subway, remain isolated except when it comes to sharing space. That's not interaction. That's not the kind of communality that will grow a We Generation, much less make children feel that they belong and are trustworthy, capable, and responsible.

Individualism rather than collectivism was what I saw most when my local school board set out to close some of its surplus classrooms. For ten weeks one winter, board members went from one school gym to another, hearing submissions from the floor by parents. Each parent spoke passionately. Each argued against the injustice of closing "my" school.

Though numbers of students are declining across the district, not one parent, to my recollection, ever attempted to find consensus, or spoke about his or her willingness to give something up for the greater good. Even schools half-full were spoken of as vibrant and engaging. The self-centeredness of the adults was disheartening.

That Me-thinking, however, is all around us, making the We-thinking kids more difficult to see. It is as if the social contract is under assault, not by the kids we blame for our social problems, but by the adults who shape the world in which children live.

It is this hyperindividualism that Michael Bull, a lecturer in media and culture at the University of Sussex in the United Kingdom, is talking about when he describes how people, young and old, are using their iPods to control their personal space. We have become obsessed with shutting others out, with isolating ourselves from the public gaze.

Like sunglasses and cell phones, our earbuds tell the world "the lights are on, but we're not answering the door." The iPod is to the urbanista what the monster home is to the suburbanite: a cocoon that allows the user to define himself or herself as separate and independent. That's not a good way to build community.

All this isolation is shattering what little community remains for our children. We fear reaching out to help one another, even our neighbors. A Trillium Foundation study in 2006 found that while 87 percent of Ontario residents knew that under the law, they were supposed to report suspected child abuse to authorities, 50 percent said they would hesitate, 55 percent said it would be difficult to report someone they know well, and 44 percent said that even a casual acquaintance would be difficult to report. Fear of retribution, not knowing whom to call, uncertainty about what constitutes abuse, and a common belief that "it's none of my business" create a culture of silence. That's not what we want to be showing the kids, now, is it?

Is Anybody Out There?

Two communities . . . two cultures . . . two sets of messages for their children. The first community, I'll call Richmond. It's a well-manicured suburb with a strong residential tax base. Town council just passed a city ordinance that residents will no longer be allowed to hang laundry outside. It seems that fluttering boxers are offensive to some and depress neighborhood property values. When I read about this in my morning newspaper, I thought immediately of the consequences of such silliness: seclusion, energy waste, formality in people's neighborly interactions. It was another way to isolate ourselves in our homes and teach our children to act selfishly. There was a time when hanging laundry was an opportunity to watch our neighbors and our neighbors' kids, and to chat informally out there on our back decks.

On a recent visit to Dublin, I wandered through the back courtyard of a new urban development that was very different from Richmond. Townhouses and apartments had been jumbled together. In the common area behind were parking spaces, a children's play area, and communal laundry trees. Everyone had a porch or balcony that looked out onto the back courtyard. It felt safe. There were people watching me as I watched them.

There is another community I know. I'll call it Smithville. It's a place where a cat's birthday is a cause for celebration.

When Calvin (the cat) turned ten, and Laura-lee's daughter, Robyn, announced to all the children on her street that there was to be a birthday party that very same Saturday afternoon, seventeen children and six parents joined Robyn's family to celebrate their feline's first decade. The children brought small homemade gifts, pieces of ribbon, a bowl of milk, a can of tuna. The parents came over to admire Calvin and have a good laugh with Laura-lee. Soon there was a cake, candles, games in the front yard, and a scared kitty that hid under the veranda. It was the kind of spontaneity that comes with a community that has watched each other's children grow and probably watched each other's laundry flutter.

It is a pattern I see us struggling to create for children in most communities. Spontaneous community. But drive-throughs, banking machines, and private automobiles are breaking apart opportunities for connections in common spaces. Throughout the United Kingdom, for example, there is nostalgia for old-style pubs where old and young gather. While the adults drank a pint, the young used to watch the old and learn the art of community building. The power of gossip that glued families to one another is eroding. We need the public commons. It's there that we play witness to expressions of compassion. We hear who's ill and who's well. Who's doing with whom something that they shouldn't be doing.

On Prince Edward Island, the pastoral home of Lucy Maud Montgomery's fictional character Anne of Green Gables, people still extol the virtues of gossip: "It is every islander's God-given right to know everything about every other islander," they joke, only half in jest.

There they take gossip as seriously as death notices. You need both of these to avoid social faux pas. Recently, there was a loud and angry outcry when a local radio station was bought by a national conglomerate and stopped its daily tradition of announcing funerals sharply at 12:30 P.M. Though it may sound morbid, islanders stopped to listen. It was important to know who'd died and which funeral home to visit. After all, it was likely that you'd soon be bumping into members of the deceased's family. It would be impolite not to know the tragedy that had befallen them.

Fighting Back

Against these threats to community, we are fighting back. Just look at San Antonio, Texas, where a network of walkways on the shores of the river has revitalized the downtown core. Year round, the pedestrian walkways are chock full of people, and restaurant patios are noisy with those who like to be noticed.

In Celebration, a Disney housing development just outside Orlando, Florida, a new urbanism is helping to inspire small, chic homes built close to a downtown core, where a sense of community can be promoted. In Savannah, Georgia, heritage buildings are protected. Even condo developers must back their towers away from the street so the low-rise feeling of older streetscapes remains. In Vancouver, they stopped building new freeways a decade ago, investing instead in the redevelopment of their inner city and public transit.

Perhaps we're not as lost as we seem. We know something is amiss for our children. Even as we expand into the suburbs and build monstrous homes, we seem to know we want more than square footage. We want our children to know connections, to people and their people's history.

Young People Can and Should Contribute

Connections are made and strengthened when we help each other. Create opportunities in our communities for participation, and our kids will surprise us with what they can do.

Skeptical? That's not surprising. After all, we don't hear much about altruism among our youth. You have to look well past the front page news to find expositions on the vast majority of our kids who are contributors to their communities. Like little nine-year-old Alyson, who is a book-buddy at school, tutoring a six-year-old one morning a week. She also enjoys fund-raising and was the one who pushed her father into bringing the family pet on a walkathon to raise money for their local animal shelter. At Easter, she makes her own cards and sells them to raise money for an overseas orphanage. Summers, she invites to her family cottage a girl who moved to her community from China. Guoxiu is just learning about canoes, barbecues, and campfire songs sung while chewing burnt marshmallows.

Kids want to be a part of their communities in meaningful ways, to participate and feel the respect that comes with helping others. It is enlightened self-interest and a formula for personal development. But it takes a community of concerned adults to create the spaces where kids shine.

Even kids who get into trouble want the same kinds of experiences Alyson has had. Brianna was lucky to have those opportunities despite becoming a mother at seventeen. Her boyfriend left her with their six-month-old son to raise alone. Her parents are understandably angry. Amid the confusion of dashed dreams for their daughter's future (or so they think) and a desire to love their grandchild, they ride an emotional roller coaster.

Brianna's future would be bleak if not for two things: first, a community of concern that has come forward to help; and second, Brianna's desire to contribute not just to her child's welfare but to her community as well. Brianna understands she has to help herself, then help others.

I was only a bit player in all this. Brianna didn't need a counselor; she needed the informal supports that come when a congregation decides that no child will be left behind. When I ask Brianna how she's been coping, she tells me, "The ladies at the church came around with lots of clothes for my baby, and a playpen and crib. I had more outfits than I needed. And everybody told me how beautiful my son is." She giggles. Holding her son, fed and clean, Brianna seems to have taken the compassion shown to her and passed it to her son.

But it wasn't just her church's ladies' auxiliary that helped. "My guidance counselor right now at my school, he's been my teacher all year. Once I had my son, it was really hard to get to school every day and to do well and stuff. But he understood. At first I had a big attitude when I came, and was, like, waiting for him and the other teachers to say something mean about what I'd done. None of them did, of course. But still, I think I was a bit embarrassed, and one day, I decided I wasn't going to come to school no more and I told my teacher, Mr. Rainforth, and he just said that everything was going to be okay if I made it okay, and that he would help me every day to get to school. That meant a lot. Because my parents were just expecting me to drop out now that I had my son." Brianna stops to resettle the baby on her lap. Then stops smiling. A question forms on her lips, but she never speaks it. I wonder if she was going to ask if that's normal. If all parents give up on their daughters if they make a mistake. If one can call a beautiful baby boy a mistake.

I anticipate the unspoken and tell her, "You've certainly shown that you have a future. You're still in school. You're raising your child. I frankly don't know how you cope. I was older and more settled when my wife and I had our first child. And even then, we were completely exhausted by it all."

"Oh, I get plenty tired," Brianna tells me, and we both laugh. It's a joke between adults, a role Brianna can share now. I realize suddenly that Brianna likes this new role, even if it wasn't chosen.

"But I couldn't get by without my guidance counselor. Even more than my parents. He sometimes picks me up and takes me to school, days my mom says she'll look after the baby. And Mr. Rainforth, he'll phone me in the morning to check if I'm coming to school. He even arranged with the school to give me bus tickets so that if I miss my bus, I can still get there. And he bought my son a sled so when there's snow I can take him with me outside. He just keeps telling me, 'It's gonna be okay,' and I believe him. If he wasn't there I would have just probably dropped out. Which is what my parents expected."

Brianna doesn't just take from her community. A member of the We Generation, she also gives back. She volunteers to coach other pregnant teens through her church. She has been giving speeches to professional groups about teen moms and their right to an education. She even wrote a poem about her life that was published in her parish newsletter.

Her challenges aren't weighing her down. They're mobilizing her strengths.

What makes all this possible is a community of concern. Brianna is strong because her community makes space for her. When communities open doors to those who are vulnerable, they do a big favor for everyone. With inclusion comes contribution.

Exclusion creates conflict, social unrest, dependency. Brianna fights these negative forces every day. Like the day I meet her and another teen mom on the subway with their children. Both mothers are pushing strollers. It's busy. There are no seats, but neither young woman seems to mind. They stand chatting and giggling like schoolgirls. Occasionally, they reach down to their children to adjust their hats or mitts. I can tell people are watching them. If you listen closely, you can hear the *tsk, tsk* of judgment. Three stops down the line, and a businessman in a suit needs to exit. He doesn't say, "Excuse me." Instead, he steps over Brianna's son and his stroller, his foot gliding close to the child's head. Brianna loses it.

"Hey!" she shouts. "What the f——do you think you're doing? That's my kid you just about stepped on." The man hardly gives her a look. Just waves a hand in her direction and keeps walking. A few of the other passengers try not to stare but are. I think they blame Brianna for the problem. I can hear them thinking, See how rude she is. I can see why she has a kid.

I think of the years I traveled with my children in strollers. No one ever stepped over them; no one would have dared. People always asked to pass, gently helping me move the stroller if necessary. They deferred to me and the important role I assumed as a parent.

It's remarkable that young women like Brianna don't sink into a steady state of anger and withdrawal. What I witnessed is only a minute of her life. She'll experience many more such moments on her way home every day, her role of mother diminished by a selfish culture that promotes individualism. Brianna talks back to those values. She is making her contribution. Unintended or otherwise, she has found her way to be a We-thinker. Mother, activist, youth . . . she is all three at once.

The City Commons

Jane Jacobs, herself an activist, an urbanite, and a parent, was the author of the American classic *The Death and Life of Great American Cities*.[2] Jacobs did more than anyone else to raise our consciousness about the communal nature of our cities. Her work awoke in urban planners a sense of something overlooked: the social capital of the city street. Where once we saw only chaos and danger, Jacobs helped show that the city street is safe because it is populated by many. It is not something to be feared. What are dangerous are the anonymous high-rises and sterile parklands that sit without the benefit of public gaze. It's amid towers of stone, steel, and glass, where people are invisible, that we lose our children to gangs and violence. That is what happens when we put people into boxes that have no porches, no collective commons.

Jacobs showed us that if we want a We Generation, we aren't going to find it easily amid the postage-stamp lots and monster homes of planned communities where cars isolate us from one another. Nor are we going to find it in high-rise apartments and condos with more villagers than many a country town.

Neighborhoods need integration. They need places our children can connect. A more communal city block with a small corner store that sells nickel candies and storefront community service agencies, next to bus routes and within walking distance of schools and places of worship, is not just a quaint urban vision. It will save our children. It will squash urban violence. When those of means live a little closer to those who live without, a culture of compassion grows. Those "others" become known. There are opportunities to give and take.

In Jacobs's world, according to her unofficial biographer, Alice Sparberg Alexiou, "people hung out on the sidewalks, where you could see them. You never felt alone there; it was a real community, a place where people both worked and played and socialized with each other."[3] The village commons only exists when we create it. If we want our children to learn about the village, we need to give them one to live in.

It's no surprise to sociologists, urban planners, social workers, anthropologists, or psychologists that we get problem slums when we remove the organic city street, with its natural integration of multiple zones of interaction. I'm not talking a return to jumbled urban poverty. Desperation doesn't create healthy interactions. But interaction lets us know each other and ultimately, selfishly, keeps us all a little safer.

If we ever got this right, we would raise children in mixed communities that were economically diverse, with housing of different shapes and sizes, where there were public spaces that people shared and where people felt a responsibility for their neighbors' welfare. Maybe the residents would even have some nostalgia for their home turfs. Can anyone really imagine children of the ubiquitous transient suburbs sitting around kitchen tables three decades from now reminiscing about their wonderful homes in wonderful communities that were full of opportunities for adventure? We have mostly killed such Huck Finn–like dreams.

If we lament the next generation's behavior, perhaps we need to ask ourselves if our loss of that simple utopia is why our children appear to be such individuals.

We haven't built them their village.

The Little Village That Could

Our children's villages have to match their size. Just like the story of Goldilocks and the three bears, the small child needs a world that fits a small child. That means a community the size of a city block. Maybe a bit bigger, if you add a community recreation center, a park with a tall slide, a doctor's office, and a nice breakfast place where parents can meet over coffee and cinnamon buns.

The older child needs a sense of place that is ten blocks by ten blocks. Boundaries that are knowable. A nearby school and friends within an easy walk, or a short drive. Preferably some rough, undeveloped space where adventure is found in trees and with leftover building supplies. A place to play tag, knock together a fort, or hide from a bully.

By the time our children are adolescents, their worlds become their cities. They'll be able to understand their place in that city if they have grown up navigating wider and wider territory. When Melissa, now seventeen, makes her way from her parents' shared living space in her cohousing unit, she is at ease. Melissa is a robust young woman who, when I met her, was tired from having attended a debating tournament at her school the night before. She'd have rested except she was expected to attend a meeting in preparation for her role in a model United Nations (she was going to play the

230 — the we generation

ambassador of Zambia). As if that wasn't enough, she was having to consider the logistics of attending a protest rally the next day. I was visiting Melissa's parents when she came in to say hello and to ask permission to go.

"Mom, can I go to the homeless protest tomorrow?" she asked. "It's in front of the government offices downtown."

Her mother, Gail, a strong advocate for the rights of youth and a health practitioner in a community clinic, seemed to take the request as just another typical moment in her daughter's life. Like being asked for permission to go on a sleepover.

"Will there be anyone with sticks hitting people? Have you checked to see if there will be tear gas?" Gail asked.

"I don't think so," Melissa said. "It's supposed to be a peaceful demonstration."

"And who's organizing it?" Gail asked. Melissa thought for a moment, then provided her mother with a verbal organizational flow chart of peace activists and poverty advocates in a city known for both its charity and its lack of government intervention, planning, or taxation.

"It doesn't sound like a problem. You're sure you won't get arrested?"

"Mom!" Melissa winced. "How can I be sure of something like that? It's a protest!" She rolled her eyes, half in jest. She knew her mother was just trying to reassure herself.

Gail pondered this a moment. She shared with me a short story of her own youthful spate of social actions and then told Melissa, "Well, then, as long as you remember to leave the protest if things get out of hand. I don't want anyone beating you up. I guess jail wouldn't be so bad. You are, after all, still a minor. You'd have no record. But be sure to call if you need a lift home afterward." I'm not sure if Gail meant from jail, or the protest, but it didn't seem to matter. Melissa knew her mother was there for her. She would have been shocked if her mother had said no. Little villages seem to create this spirit of We. That village can be a Jane Jacobs–size city block or a cohousing collective. It can be a school classroom or a sports team. But the common element among communities that cope well is their capacity to respond when adversity strikes. A community that works is one where each person, young or old, feels a sense of place and purpose in that community. There is mutual and assured dependency.

The remarkable thing is how often it is our children out front, leading us into community rather than following. Nowhere is this so evident than in stories told by the "lost boys of Sudan," 27,000 youngsters who were forced to flee their homes and families in southern Sudan because of a genocidal government decree that all males were to be killed. After a thousand miles of marching through desert and forest, the boys eventually found shelter in a refugee camp in Northern Kenya, where they lived for the next decade. Pictures of their plight would move a few nations to extend them refugee status. Many of the boys were sponsored by church groups and found their way to North America and Europe. In the movie *God Grew Tired of Us*, narrated by Nicole Kidman and produced by the National Geographic Society, the story of several of the lost boys is told.

What is so compelling about these boys' stories is that those who could help others, did. They formed their own nomadic families. If one boy was particularly tall, or an uncle to other smaller boys, then he became the family head. The boys had a strong desire to lead and to take the roles given them. Even after the boys reached their new homes in the

West, many continued to do everything they could to make life better for those who had been less fortunate (including working very long hours at minimum wage and sending the money back to the camp). The boys insist people need to stay connected. Their culture compels them to look after the others they left behind.

Our Children Are Watching

In Montreal, an all-Jewish radio station broadcasts programming six days a week for the large Jewish community of the city. There are talk shows, music, and entertainment reviews. On Saturdays, the Sabbath, the radio station goes silent for its Jewish listeners, as befits a religious enterprise. Each Saturday, though, the station is taken over by an evangelical Christian group that broadcasts its shows for the day.

It is an odd shared arrangement between two peoples who have not always been good neighbors. It is the kind of thing that happens when community is present.

Our children are watching.

We see lots of strange partnerships when we look for hopeful signs of community that will inspire our children to behave with tolerance and compassion. Bill Gates, chairman of Microsoft and billionaire philanthropist, says business, universities, and social advocates need closer ties. Business can be the machinery of change. As the Bill & Melinda Gates Foundation is demonstrating, profits can be turned into ploughshares, medicine, research, and lifesaving interventions for those without means. AIDS, malaria, and homelessness are just some of the issues that the private sector seems to be tackling with aplomb in the absence of sufficient government will.

Our children are watching.

For decades, John McKnight has been working in Chicago and across North America to deprofessionalize health care. He has shown that communities are often the best source of healing, not the professionals paid to service them. Where professionals think in terms of the eventual termination of service, communities think of transitions: movement from formal helping systems to informal community supports. That's where we all come in. The grieving parent whose child dies in a car accident, the child recovering from lymphoma, the senior with dementia who wants to stay in his own home, all offer opportunities for their neighbors to rally support and build community.

Our children are watching.

Our children can be coached to lead us into community. In fact, if we listen to leaders like Michael Brown, CEO of the Bronx's City Year and cofounder of the Young Heroes Program, we'll hear that kids are keen to make a contribution when adults provide the opportunities. "We need to spark a sense of civic identity in young people and turn them on to being citizens," says Brown. Coast to coast, Young Heroes provides middle-school students the chance to do volunteer work in their communities. They form groups that address social issues such as AIDS, homelessness, and hunger. Run by young people themselves, the Young Heroes Program reaches deep into communities to offer volunteer contributions where help is needed most.[4] Such efforts don't need much priming, but they do need guidance from us adults.

Our children are watching.

Children will give up self-destructive behaviors when their communities model for them collective solutions. Chris Lalonde and his colleague Marc Chandler on Canada's West Coast wanted to understand better the loss of identity that many have speculated contributes to world-record levels of teen suicide among youth in Canada's Native communities.[5] It's a problem for non-Native youth as well, though on a lesser scale. Comparing 196 Native communities over fourteen years, Lalonde and Chandler show that youth suicide disappears as a social problem when communities provide their kids with continuity of culture and a sense of pride of place:

> The surprising outcomes—the transcendence—is not found in the single "hardy" or "invulnerable" child who manages to rise above adversity, but in the existence of whole communities that demonstrate the power of culture as a protective factor. When communities succeed in promoting their cultural heritage and in securing control of their own collective future—in claiming ownership over their past and future—the positive effects reverberate across many measures of youth health and well-being. Suicide rates fall, fewer children are taken into care, school completion rates rise, and rates of intentional and unintentional injury decrease.[6]

Our children are watching.

Indeed, around the world, strong communities of compassionate adults are raising strong children by modeling for them how to live in community.

Happiness Through Connection

There is a fable about a huckster who traveled from village to village making soup from a stone. It was a time when many travelers pestered townspeople and when townspeople themselves seldom trusted one another. Understanding this, the huckster's approach was simple. He would enter each town and approach the first door that showed promise of being opened. The stranger, insisting he was not a beggar, would show whomever opened her door a hefty white stone that he pulled from his satchel and explain that he could make soup from it. He needed only to borrow a pot of water for boiling, a ladle, and a few sticks to make his fire. Such a simple request would inevitably be granted by the home-owner, as much out of curiosity as kindness. Shortly, there would be a roaring fire and a boiling pot of water. When the woman (or man) and neighbors came to see what the man had accomplished, he would delicately taste his soup and then exclaim, "Ah, so fine! But a few herbs would certainly make my soup perfect." Again, such a small request was easy enough to grant, and soon another householder would have brought a snippet of thyme, sage, or dill. Again the soup was tasted, and again the huckster said, "Ah, so fine! But a few potatoes, that is what it needs to be perfect." Once the pota-toes had been added, the next request was for a carrot, then a turnip, then a small meat bone left over from an earlier feast. It wasn't long before the huckster did indeed have his fine soup, and more than enough to share with the towns-people. It was then that he let them taste his creation. The story ends with the townspeople marveling at the miracle of the huckster's hearth and a stone that can make soup.

Of course, the story teaches us about social capital. In the early 1990s, Robert D. Putman wrote that the density of population and level of civic participation (voting, volun-teerism, community events), among other aspects of society, create civility and drive economic growth. Putman's most popular book, *Bowling Alone*, was a remarkably insightful look at the foundations of our society: the "stones" that bring us together and make the sum of our individual participation greater than what we could accomplish on our own.[7]

Similarly, Peter L. Benson, the founder of Search Institute, tells us that kids do best when there is a community to look after them. In his book *All Kids Are Our Kids*, Benson provides a list of the dream qualities every community needs if it's to raise a healthy next generation:

- Daily doses of care and support provided by one or more very involved, loving parents or other substitute caregivers
- Sustained relationships with adults who are other than the child's parent
- A neighborhood where everyone knows, protects, listens to, and gets involved with the kids
- Opportunities for kids to participate in developmentally challenging clubs, teams, and organizations that are led by principled, responsible, and trained adults
- Access to child-friendly public places
- Daily affirmation and encouragement
- Relationships between the generations that let children and teenagers bond with adults, and older children relate to younger ones
- A stake in community life based on meaningful roles that allow young people to be involved
- Appropriate boundaries, prosocial values, and reasonable expectations that adults articulate to the kids and model in their own lives
- Peer groups that encourage kids to achieve and contribute

- Caring schools, congregations, and other youth-serving organizations
- Opportunities for kids to be givers rather than just takers[8]

Every community is going to define "appropriate" participation, values, and contributions for its young people. In fact, agreeing on these definitions was one of the biggest sticking points when the United Nations negotiated with its member states the Convention on the Rights of the Child. Different cultures see children very differently. Some societies would never tolerate outspoken children questioning their parents' authority. Others would never allow children to be coddled and protected well into adolescence, insisting they be allowed to work in family-run businesses or on farms. Every culture, however, has a vision of how and when a young person should become a successful adult. All can describe in detail the role adults are expected to play to ensure that tyrannical four-year-olds become nicely behaved fourteen-year-olds and competent, compassionate twenty-four-year-old contributors to the welfare of others. When adults fail, when the structures we provide (our houses, schools, and city streets) isolate, discriminate, and demotivate, we get Me-thinking packs of youths roaming without any adults to guide their development.

From a Child's Point of View

Child by child, we can see the practical difference social capital makes in the lives of our children. A year ago, I was asked to assess the living situation of a nine-year-old boy named Joshua whose mother was petitioning the court for sole custody of her son. What was remarkable about this relatively common scenario is that in this case, I found myself assessing not just the child and the child's relationship with each of his parents, but also the social capital of each community in which he would live.

Joshua is a rocket. He plays hockey every chance he gets. He attends hockey summer camps when you'd think a child would be more interested in swimming outdoors underwater than skating across it in an indoor rink.

Joshua has had a pretty good life despite his parents' divorce when he was two. His mother works part-time administration jobs; his father is a manager of a home renovation store. The father has been remarried for a number of years, and Joshua gets along well with his stepmother and younger stepsister. Week on, week off, Joshua has moved back and forth between his two homes with little stress. His parents cooperated as best they could, though it was his father who made sure Joshua got to every hockey game. However, when Joshua's mother met her new partner living half a province away, a decision had to be made. Place Joshua with his mother almost full-time, or let him stay with his father and visit his mother every second weekend and holidays. Both homes were adequate. Both parents wanted what was best for Joshua. Joshua just wanted to stay put, in his old school, playing hockey with the friends he'd had since he'd started skating at age three.

I met with every member of the family. I visited Joshua at both homes. He seemed to prefer his room at his father's, where Joshua had decorated the walls with posters of all the great forwards of the NHL. At school, I heard about an average student who was athletic and friendly. I even went to see him play at an exhibition game against an out-of-province team. Joshua scored in the first half, and you could hear his father cheering from across the rink. I watched the way the other boys patted him on the back and the closeness he experienced with his coach, who thumped him gently on his helmet as he did his victory lap after the goal. It was a good game even if Joshua's team lost, 3 to 2.

I eventually recommended that Joshua remain with his father. Raising Joshua was about more than just what each parent could give the boy. It was about what his community gave him, too. I wasn't really concerned with whether Joshua would get a chance to play hockey in his new town. He would. I was concerned that Joshua would lose the continuity of the attachments he already had with a whole host of concerned adults and peers. In my heart, despite his mother's tears when I explained what I was going to recommend to the court, I just couldn't think of Joshua as the sole responsibility of his parents to raise.

Children Want to Join In

Peter L. Benson reminds us that our children need, and want, to be a part of their communities, but there is much working against this integration, including what he describes as the "cancerous spread of age segregation, in which adults and children go their separate ways. The architecture and design of communities and neighborhoods isolates families, and virtually every program and institution is organized to meet age-specific needs at the expense of the richness of intergenerational community. The public perception of danger and the rise of mistrust freezes connectedness and undermines community."[9]

Utopian-community proponents like Benson inspire a sense of "we-ness." You can actually see these communities at work creating inclusion. There is measurably more to-getherness, more days spent in each other's company, and the perceptions by one group (adults) of other groups (teenagers) are positive and inclusive. The community func-tions because it understands itself to be a group. These inter-actions build bridges between individuals. Both Joshua and his dad traveled such bridges.

The great thing about bridge building is that sometimes our kids are the builders, for themselves and their parents. All those sporting events, birthday parties, and school con-certs influence the number of positive connections parents experience. In this sense, children can influence the well-being of adults. Such an inversion of responsibility reminds me of a story I once heard about a truck that had become wedged in the mouth of a tunnel leading into New York City. It was sandwiched between the asphalt below and the ce-ment above. Slowly, traffic was diverted around the vehicle while the tow trucks and police tried to back it out. It was a little boy, I heard, who shouted out his car window as he drove by, "Why don't you deflate the tires?" With some cha-grin, the adults listened and the problem was solved.

Maybe that story is an urban myth, but solving our chil-dren's need for connections is not an adult responsibility alone. Children, too, have something to offer.

In the search for relationships, children like Joshua want to feel a part of their communities. Regardless if he's a Triple A goal-scoring hockey star or a dependable defenseman on a house league team, a child who knows he has a place and purpose in his village is going to do better than one who does not.

This truth obligates us all to create the social networks that convey to our community's children they belong. There are many small gestures that cumulatively make a difference:

- Paying attention to children
- Getting to know them by name
- Asking them for a favor
- Challenging them with responsibility
- Encouraging them to try something new
- Expecting something of them
- Letting them teach you a song
- Asking them about themselves
- Offering to play with them
- Delighting in what they discover
- Laughing at their jokes
- Getting to know their friends
- Making sure they know that you accept and love them, unconditionally

When Children Play Their Part

Give our children half a chance to be a part of our communities, and most will gladly accept the invitation. They'll even lead. As Marc and Craig Kielburger write in *Take Action!* their guide to active citizenship, "Each one of us has the potential to change the world. It does not matter where you live or how old you are—your contributions are important and can help promote change."[10] The members of this next generation will be the one to address global warming and the problems of salinity changes in the oceans, fish stock depletion, and freshwater shortages. They are interested in the AIDS epidemic and concerned about the toxicity of suburban lawns. They listen when rock stars talk about white-skinned beluga whales whose flesh is so polluted with heavy metals that disposing of a carcass requires handling the remains as toxic waste. That curiosity about their world comes from feeling a part of it. When bombs are dropped on the people of Afghanistan, and "collateral damage" results in the death of schoolchildren, the images our children see on the evening news make the lives of those others less anonymous.

Our children define their village on a global scale. Our villages, though, are still only as good as the governments that run them and make them family-friendly. I'm not ideological in this regard. If tax breaks for businesses that contribute to building skateboard parks make my community safer, then I'm okay with that. If higher property taxes mean public transit and swimming pools that poor families can afford, then I'm a pragmatist and will lend my support. After all, I want to feel safe. My actions are part compassion, part self-interest. Bill me the few extra bucks. It's still cheaper than a house alarm, a private police force, or the emotional pain of watching a loved one assaulted.

Youth who feel a part of their communities are less likely to vandalize it. Less likely to be violent. More likely to stay in school and work. More likely to act responsibly.

If we really want our families to raise responsible kids, then we have to make sure that families have what they need to do the job. The more integrated our communities are, the more that our schools have the same standards and resources rather than a patchwork of municipal charity, then the more likely we'll have kids with the skills to give back to their communities. It's up to us older villagers to make it all possible.

Tips List

The We-thinking child starts early to give back, and then keeps on giving. Though it's never too late to instill in our children a sense of We, starting earlier makes the job easier.

Think back to when you were a child. Ask yourself, In what ways was I expected to make a contribution to my family, school, and community? Write these activities down, or even better, talk to your child about what you were doing when you were the same age as your child is now.

Over the years, I've heard from different parents a variety of stories about the contributions they made. I've also heard from them lots of great ideas about how they've encouraged their own children to participate more. Here are some of the strategies parents have shared with me that they use to encourage their children to show responsibility for themselves and others as they grow older.

When children are under five, they can

- help bake and do other household chores, like take out garbage and tidy their rooms;
- decide on activities they'd like to do, and ask politely to do them;
- learn to say thank you and be responsible for acknowledging gifts at birthdays and holidays;
- learn to share their toys, or pick out old toys and donate them.

Between ages five and eleven, children can
- have responsibility for a younger sibling's care;
- look after a pet;
- learn to use "dangerous toys" like pocket knives and push scooters;
- decide what they'll wear to school;
- walk themselves to school (where appropriate).

In junior and senior high, children can
- become certified as lifeguards or junior coaches;
- volunteer or seek paid work;
- learn how to use power tools and lawnmowers;
- accept responsibility for what they wear, and contribute money toward their purchases;
- plan events at school like a dance or graduation;
- participate in religious or spiritual ceremonies that mark their transition to adulthood.

CONCLUSION
We-Thinkers

In New Zealand, children in elementary school take turns as crossing guards. Under the supervision of an adult, teams of three kids sport bright yellow vests and get to operate stop signs attached to metal booms that are swung out into intersections to stop traffic. What child wouldn't like to be a crossing guard? There is such power in making adults stop. It is real power exercised for the benefit of others—a social role that brings with it genuine respect. It is the kind of self-esteem booster on which a We Generation thrives.

Contrast that with the obnoxious child who insists she play forward for her soccer team and no other position. She pouts and refuses to listen to her coach who encourages her to play defense, where her big kicks and rough-and-tumble ways are needed by the team. Her parents will have none of the coach's suggestions. They stopwatch every minute their daughter is on the field. They insist she play as much as or more than every other child. They declare that if their daughter wants to play forward, then she should be given the chance to play forward, even if her ball-handling skills need work and her team is not as likely to win as a consequence.

Enlightened self-esteem is the feeling we give our children when what they have to offer finds a niche among their families and communities. That's a formula for feeling the sense of cohesion that comes with being a contributing part of others' lives. The self-centered bully doesn't know that feeling.

Enlightened self-esteem develops character. As General Norman Schwarzkopf ("Stormin' Norman," as he was known during his time as commander in chief of coalition forces for the 1991 Iraq War) said, "If I had to go into battle with a strategy or character, I'd choose character."

The opportunities for our children to develop character are all around us. Walk into most elementary schools, and you are likely to find desks grouped in pods and teachers instructing children in the finer points of collaboration. Our educators are doing a lot these days to raise a generation of We-thinkers. They are creating a learning environment that conveys a positive school culture, pride of place, and sensitivity to ethnocultural differences. There are fund-raisers for the less fortunate and letter-writing campaigns to complain about injustices. Any parent of a school-age child knows that most schools see it as their role to awaken in children compassion for the needs of others. Our children accept the offer when it brings with it an awareness of themselves as givers, rather than takers. That's the basis for enlightened self-esteem: experiences of helping others that are genuinely effective.

It's the same for our little ones at home. Ask yourself, What does dinner time look like at my house? Are your kids obligated to help? To cook? To set the table? Did they help put away the groceries? Empty the dishwasher? Put out the compost?

Or are dinners a testament to a "Give me" culture. Have your children become spoiled like Paris Hilton? Arrogant like rap star Soulja Boy? As petulant as Britney Spears? Or are they more like rock star and international aid activist Bono? Or the UN High Commission for Refugees goodwill ambassador Angelina Jolie? There is within our children a desire to do for others rather than to have everything done for themselves. Without opportunities to show themselves as We-thinkers and the expectations that they will make a contribution, many children risk becoming nothing more than selfish individuals distracted by privilege.

Growing a Generation to Be Proud Of

A remarkable project called Kids Company, led by social entrepreneur Camila Batmanghelidjh in London's inner city, offers emotionally withdrawn and neglected youths a way to navigate back into the social fabrics of their communities and schools. Batmanghelidjh understands kids. Faced with chronic exposure to the trauma of inner-city life, kids protest, she says. They shut down their feelings. This numb state of "I don't care" is a refutation of everything we think they should be. But then again, these kids are growing up with no allegiance to civil society because, as Batmanghelidjh explains, civil society abandoned them long ago.

Kids Company reverses children's pathways into the anomie of London's street youth culture. Caring adults trained in psychoanalysis work closely with children of the poorest communities, some 10,000 kids in thirty-three schools, conveying to them compassion for their feelings. The magic is in the continuity each therapist provides. Through proximity with someone who genuinely cares, children are reparented. They find someone who understands they are victims even as they victimize others. They are offered a way to again become part of the weave of relationships that tell them they count. Batmanghelidjh's work gives us cause for optimism: Kids can be saved.

I find just as much cause for hope among the kids themselves when I look. During an interview with Barbara Walters prior to the 2008 Academy Awards, Ellen Page talked about her controversial role as a pregnant teenager in the movie *Juno*. Her performance earned her a nomination for Best Actress and made many parents wonder whether young people today are too quick to celebrate what to parents' minds is a big problem (the movie does not, however, promote teenage pregnancy). Walters asked Page if she thought it was realistic that the girl she plays, Juno, would really be able to go to school, nine months pregnant, and get so little abuse from her classmates. "Sure," Page answered, "kids today aren't so bad." Like Batmanghelidjh, Page, too, knows that young people are more tolerant than we give them credit for.

Idiot Compassion

There are many families whose children will never know the street life of the inner-city child, yet are still at risk of emotional deprivation. The danger for us middle-class parents is that for everything we do right, we may jeopardize our children's welfare through displays of what Buddhists call "idiot compassion." Overprotection, big houses, material excess, long commutes to boring jobs that we complain about at dinner, overly structured playtimes for our kids, and other diseases of modernity aren't teaching our children about the value of connections with others. We think we are looking after our children, when in fact we are teaching them how to become self-centered, valuing the satiation of their own needs instead of the quality of their connections with others.

A disturbing trend among North American adults is that we don't take our full allotment of vacation time. Parents who don't take their vacation time run the risk of starving their children of what they really need while force-feeding them a diet of material distractions. Rising rates of workaholism pay homage to the god of avarice and the myth of productivity (fewer vacation days in the United States does not mean higher productivity). We are working harder but not teaching our children about the value of our labor or the intrinsic value of family and commitment.

My worry is we'll soon need Kids Company for the over-privileged.

Keeping in mind that our children are watching us for clues about how to connect, the father who is not taking his vacation time is likely to be telling his children they don't really matter. That they are not worth as much as an extra day's pay or a new car.

After all, vacation time isn't just about down time or amusement parks. It's about the connections we make while being present to our kids. A driving holiday is as likely to be full of sniveling, angry outbursts, and pleas to go home as it is to be the source of frequent sing-alongs, shared meals at family restaurants, and the occasional playful tussle on a beach. Yet the advantages almost always outweigh the costs.

We need to ask ourselves whether all that work we're doing is getting us and our children what we really need. When it comes to creating a We Generation, the family with the most toys doesn't necessarily win. It's about balance. In 2006, more than 88,000 iPods were sold each day in the United Sates. So too were 35 million cans of Bud Light and

628 Toyota Camrys. Add to that 70,000 kilograms of Starbucks coffee, and we quickly see we are good at buying things.[1]

But is all our wealth making us better connected? Happier?

Well-being comes from genuine connections and the mutual dependencies that large homes and suburbs struggle to promote. The wealthiest of our neighborhoods are also those most vulnerable to the ills associated with low-context communities, places where people seldom know their neighbors and count on no one but themselves. Residents suffer from a lack of cohesiveness and an apathy toward the greater good. NIMBY-ism, the ubiquitous "not in my backyard" prejudice that ignores responsibility for others, is symptomatic of communities torn asunder by wealth. When it comes to raising children amid affluence, it's wise to remember "Buyers beware!"

Invitations

When my local town council established a committee to look at building an underage chem-free club next to a downtown park, the youth were invited to the meetings along with other community members. The kids went on and on about how much they needed this place. It was where they could perform music and hang out on Saturday nights. If you listened closely, you could hear them begging for a place where they could see and be seen.

Parents were concerned about violence and drugs. A clubhouse would attract problems, they said. With some artful facilitation, both sides got heard. No clubhouse was built, but a corner of the park was given over to outdoor evening concerts, weather permitting. Youth bands would have their showcase, and the kids would be outdoors, visible to their community. Sure, there would be noise problems, maybe drinking and drugs, but when it came right down to it, those problems had always been there. Shyly, many of the parents who had been the most vocal about the nuisance the evening concerts would cause admitted they once hung out in that very same park drinking till all hours.

Extend the invitation, and kids will come. They will speak. They will offer their advice on contentious municipal issues. That's because our kids want to impress. Behind the bravado of independence is their need for connections. Want proof? Organizations with whom I partner locally routinely invite young people (even the petty delinquent, the dropout, the kid cleaning windshields for coins at a busy intersection, the graffiti artist, the hash fiend from out behind the high school, and the party girl) to community meetings like the one just mentioned. The kids almost always come when they feel they'll have a say over issues like concerts, the design of a new skateboard park, the location of the new high school, or laws governing panhandling. They may arrive bedraggled, with attitude, and insensitive to the need to maintain order and decorum, but they come nonetheless. They sit there, happy, and express their opinions. As long as what we ask them is of concern to them, they will let themselves become engaged.

In a community where I once lived, the kids were excited about getting an extreme skateboard park, a BMX track, and a pool built. The adults were thinking more along the lines of tennis courts and walking trails until they heard from the kids. I liked what the kids had to say. My vote was for fewer tennis courts and more extreme-sports facilities. Thinking about it from the kids' point of view, I knew they wanted places where kids can watch kids. I'd suggested keeping the whole design very public, for instance, making sure the walking trails (some were still planned) went close to the BMX track. That way, the kids would feel that they were part of the community. It would be better if there were lots of passersby watching. Kids love the opportunity to put on a show.

Invitations work if we convey to kids that they are an important part of their communities, that they too are citizens and have a part to play in their families, their neighborhoods, and the global village. That's what youth themselves say. In fact, when Daniel Perkins from Pennsylvania State University and his colleagues set out to understand why young people join youth programming, the researchers found lots of reasons for and against participation. In one study of minority youths, who are often thought to be less likely to join structured activities, Perkins heard that youth participate for various reasons:

- To avoid the streets and dangerous influences
- To learn new things
- To avoid boredom
- To have fun
- To learn life skills
- To be with friends
- To get help with schoolwork
- To feel accepted[2]

It's not good enough to offer an open gym late at night if the rules and atmosphere make it uncool to be there. There's no point inviting kids to help design a recreation center if they have no real say in what it will look like. The more we let kids influence programming, negotiating with adults for what they want, the more likely they are to take us up on our offer and swap the street for the center.

Changing Landscapes of Connections

This We Generation is forcing parents to change their expectations as their children change the landscape of their connections. Our kids are breaking down barriers. They are seeking new identities that don't jibe well with the individualism of their parents. Whatever we may think about white kids watching Black Entertainment Television, or Native American kids denying their cultural heritage to appear more white, the fact is that our kids' lives are beginning to look like Benetton clothing ads: a pastiche of different skin colors and cultures with their own tribal customs. They use netspeak (that strange language used to send text messages), listen to world music (with its infusion of pop, rock, African, Latino, jazz, and classical rhythms), and think of shopping as a virtual experience.

As I survey the terrain, my optimism grows. When families take responsibility to prepare their children to navigate these new contested territories where cultures collide, children do just fine. In this world that is slowly losing its color coding, our children are the vanguards of a new tolerance for complexity. Families do many things to prepare their children for participation in this global schmooze. Travel is one way to help them understand differences, and there are many other ways: hosting exchange students; using the Internet wisely; supporting local events that promote diversity, such as street festivals, concerts, and cultural awareness months; reading books by authors from around the world; scattering news magazines around the house, both mainstream publications like *Time* and *Maclean's* and their more alternative cousins like *Utne* and *Mother Jones*; fund-raising to support people in less fortunate circumstances, whether across town or on another continent; talking about cultural differences over dinner (while eating with chopsticks or your hands); or exploring the economics of a cup of coffee over dessert.

We will need to teach children how to use and filter the information they get through their multimedia universes and realize that all news is biased one way or another. We are still our children's teachers, no matter how different the rules appear to be from the ones we played by at their age.

My focus on people and our relationships doesn't mean I'm a Luddite when it comes to all that newfangled gadgetry. I have no illusion that our lives were better before BlackBerries and iPhones. I like my toys, and my children love the zing of watching YouTube blunders and posting their lives on Facebook. I communicate weekly with my research colleagues on every continent (except Antarctica), maintain a listserv of hundreds of names, and feel intimately involved with friends whom I see face-to-face only rarely.

Ours is a world of global connections. But those connections mean little unless we understand what it means to act compassionately toward others, whether those others are in our homes or halfway around the globe.

Most exciting of all, I am learning that every adult can play a part in nurturing compassion among children. Adults such as Erin Gruwell, whose book *The Freedom Writers Diary: How a Teacher and 150 Teens Used Writing to Change Themselves and the World Around Them*, makes the point vividly. Gruwell's work in Room 203 at Woodrow Wilson High School in Long Beach, California, in 1994 helped the "unteachable" students she'd been handed to change their lives. While Hollywood's depiction of traumatized kids in Los Angeles County may have been a little sentimental, what the film adaptation, *Freedom Writers*, gets right is that young people want to find a place where they can connect. In Gruwell's classroom, they found that place and, with it, the safety and blanketlike security that they knew nowhere else, not even at home. As simple as it seems, that connection was created when they looked up at their teacher and saw someone who liked them. When she asked them to write about their lives in journals she bought with her own money, she gave them a choice. They could keep what they wrote in their journals private, or they could share what they wrote with her. They all shared.

When Kids Are Left to Find Their Own Connections

No parent gets it right all the time, and many parents who themselves grew up in homes where love was lacking still go on to make a contribution, to raise healthy families, and to participate actively as good citizens. Their success, though, is usually linked to connections with someone significant who did show them compassion.

I meet many concerned parents who vow, "I will never do to my child what was done to me." Sometimes it works. Oftentimes, it doesn't. Compassion must be learned from someone who touches us deeply. The parent who vows to be more to her child than her parents were to her still lacks a boilerplate to guide her behavior. However, the good news is that the answers are always there for us to find if we choose to look for them. We can be more than what we were shown to be when we let ourselves be inspired as parents by our children and by others in our communities.

Does being inspired by our children work? It can. Our choice is to either repeat the mistakes we were taught or to convey compassion to our children and break the cycle of emotional victimhood. Consider the very real danger posed to a lonely child who uses the Internet unsupervised. My local paper recently reported the story of a father of a thirteen-year-old who discovered that his daughter, on a dare, had lifted her shirt and let a classmate of hers see her breasts during an Internet chat. It was done as a lark, with him following suit and sending her a picture of his penis. This is the kind of stuff of which parents' nightmares are made.

Of course, the pictures circulated, and soon what was a private communication became a very public embarrassment. Dad was furious; he woke his daughter and dragged her by the hair into the computer room, slamming her head into the computer screen. He slapped her and yelled at her. Then the social workers were called, and the police. Blame was tossed back and forth. The girl was removed from the home and placed with her mother. Dad went to jail. Obviously, it didn't help that he had eleven prior convictions for violent offences.

I can't imagine that this thirteen-year-old had ever experienced much compassion. One, after all, wonders why a young woman would want to expose herself like that. I suspect she was looking for a connection. The boy at the other end of the feed wasn't anonymous; she must have known him. My guess is she wanted to find a way to excite him, to make him want to be her friend, maybe sexually. More likely, she just wanted to be accepted and known for something special she had to offer. Sadly, all she could think to share with him was the most superficial.

When our children experience our compassion and know their self-worth, they are far less likely to compromise themselves in such ways. Children raised in homes that are "good enough" have no need for the affections of sexually precocious partners or predatory adults. Psychologist Donald Winnicott says homes that are "good enough" don't have to be exceptional to work.[3] They need only be ordinary, providing enough of what our children must have to know they count.

Expanding Horizons

To parents, the We Generation poses a problem and an opportunity. Say, for example, your son wants to build a potato cannon. "What," you ask, "is that?" In this digital age, it's easy to connect your youngster to a global community of potato cannon builders. Soon you're on the Internet and downloading plans from a family in Utah, where potatoes are popular and little boys' imaginations big. A day later, you are on your back deck with the neighbors watching as your son forces a plug of raw potato down a six-foot piece of PVC plastic pipe into which has been drilled a barbecue igniter. Below the potato plug is compressed hairspray that your son had fun loading. You're thinking this looks dangerous, but you let him get everything set as safely as he can. When it's all ready, he hits the igniter and the potato plug fires high over the top of your neighbor's house and lands a full block away. Maybe a bit too much hairspray, you think, while everyone claps and whistles.

Sure, it was the Internet that made it possible to quickly and effortlessly design a potato cannon. Sure, you might feel obsolete for having not been the one to answer your child's question. But children are still children. They want our help and then they want us as their audience. No matter how seemingly big and interwoven their worlds become, it still matters to them that Dad or Mom is out on the back deck with them when they're showing off.

Watching that cannon being built reminded me that our children's world is a weave of interconnections that benefit them. It is a world that is shrinking with every online search. With a little coaching, our children can experience a sense of neighborliness with people living in any of the 192 countries that are member states of the United Nations. They can relate to the lived experience of people half a world away. Utah . . . Halifax. It can seem there is practically no distance between us. Beijing? Johannesburg? Bogotá? Those places, too, are known to our children.

Parents Count More Than Ever

Paradoxically, to survive and thrive in this world of six billion, our children are going to need the intimacy their families provide. What our children experience with us spurs their growth as compassionate and responsible young adults. I think we've forgotten this. We've misunderstood what it means to raise a child with a global perspective. It's not about technology. All that information that finds its way onto our children's computer screens is worthless unless they feel a personal sense of connection to others. What Christina, whom we met in the introduction, needs, all children need: to feel the passionate gaze of someone who loves them.

There is a popular campfire song that talks about a frog on a log in a forest. Each chorus adds another layer to the story, helping us to understand that the smallest thing is an integral part of everything much larger. Raising children today is much the same. Family life is the foundation for how children connect with others at school, in their communities, on the job, as citizens, and, finally, as members of the human race.

These connections that build community cannot be codified. They are, instead, organic. They grow from the natural interactions we share with one another. Karl Marx tried to explain that when there is abundance, our natural tendency is to care for each other as we care for ourselves. Amid such abundance, the banner greeting people at our community gate should read: "From each according to his ability, to each according to his needs!" Marx never meant for his compassionate expression of cooperation to corrupt into totalitarianism. As we have witnessed, utopian communities that try to force people to be kind to one another fail, deteriorating into oligarchies of privilege as we've seen in Russia and other "communist" states such as Laos and Romania. I doubt compassion can be legislated, measured, and mandated. It is something more offered than demanded.

And yet, will our children take the time to care for one another if that caring isn't required by law? A community that ignores the welfare of its most vulnerable will not teach its children compassion. I put little stock in the hyperindividualism and naive beneficence promoted by writers like Ayn Rand, the author of *Atlas Shrugged* and other myopic treatises on capitalism. A We Generation will not be manufactured by policy. But it also won't grow without support and modeling. If it is to exist, it will bloom because parents show their children how compassion works in the everyday arenas of family and community.

Elie Wiesel, who survived the Nazi concentration camps, concluded that there are three paths to enlightenment: devotion (the rhythmic routine of prayer and penance); suffering (experiences of great challenge and survival); and creativity (acts of creation through the arts). Our children need their parents to model at least one of these paths. These youngsters want to learn how to put into practice their devotion to a clean, more just society. Their suffering is the anxiety they experience when they are assaulted by threats of global warming and racial genocide. Their creativity is their music, dress, and tribal-like customs that convey the measure of their need to be different from generations before them. As their parents, we are being carefully assessed by them for what we can offer. If we listen closely, we will hear our children asking our permission to live their lives differently from ours. To live connected, first with us, and then with others they encounter globally.

ACKNOWLEDGMENTS

A book like this is a collaboration that relies on the wisdom of many of those with whom I have worked over the years, like Jackie Sanders and Robyn Munford, as well as those who participate in research that I lead. What I know, I have learned from those who have shared their lives with me. Often I feel more like a traveling storyteller than a family therapist. The lessons learned from one family pass to the next.

As always, much of the inspiration for this book also comes from raising my own two children, Scott and Meg, and from my partner, Cathy. It is my day-to-day connections with them, and with the many friends with whom we share our lives, that make my work what it is. A great deal of the credit for this book goes to what they have taught me.

I am deeply thankful to Wendy Francis at Da Capo Press for her encouraging words and guidance bringing this work to the United States. I have also to thank Susan Renouf, Vice President and Associate Publisher (Non-Fiction) at McClelland & Stewart, for her earlier help with this project. Elizabeth Kribs provided the very thoughtful first round of careful edits that brought out the best from the manuscript. If this book reads well, and the message is consistent, it is her doing.

I also want to thank my staff at the Resilience Research Center for their support with my many projects while I was finalizing this work. I very much appreciate the help I receive from Linda Liebenberg, Nora Didkowski, and Amber Raja.

APPENDIX

Answer Key to "How Connected Are Your Kids?" (Chapter 2)

The higher your child's score, the more aspects of positive citizenship he or she shows.

Questions	Score for Each Answer				Your Child's Score
	A	B	C	D	
1	−1	1	0	—	_____
2	−1	1	0	−1	_____
3	−1	1	0	—	_____
4	−1	1	−1	—	_____
5	−1	1	1	—	_____
6	−1	1	0	−1	_____
7	1	1	1	−1	_____
8	0	−1	1	—	_____
9	−1	1	1	—	_____
10	0	−1	1	—	_____
11	−1	−1	−1	1	_____
12	1	0	−1	—	_____
13	−1	0	1	1	_____
14	1	1	1	−1	_____
15	1	−1	0	—	_____
16	1	0	−1	—	_____
17	1	1	−1	—	_____
18	1	−1	0	—	_____
19	1	0	1	—	_____
20	1	1	0	−1	_____
21	−1	0	1	—	_____
22	0	−1	1	−1	_____
23	1	−1	1	0	_____
24	−1	1	1	—	_____
				Total	_____

NOTES

Preface

1. Most criminologists agree that today's youth are much safer than a generation ago, with lower levels of crime, drug abuse, and violence. See Chesney-Lind, M., and Irwin, K. *Beyond bad girls.* New York: Routledge; 2008. Federal Interagency Forum on Child and Family Statistics. *America's children: Key national indicators of well-being 2007.* Federal Interagency Forum on Child and Family Statistics, Washington, DC: Government Printing Office; 2007. U.S. Centers for Disease Control and Prevention. Youth risk behavior surveillance: United States, 2005. *Morbidity and Mortality Weekly Report;* 2006:55 (June 9):ss–5. Poulin, C. *Harm reduction policies and programs for youth.* Ottawa: Canadian Centre on Substance Abuse; August 2006.

Introduction

1. Hall, G.S. *Adolescence.* New York: Appleton-Century Crofts; 1904.
2. Bauman, Z. *Liquid modernity.* Cambridge, UK: Polity; 2000.
3. Lindgren, M., Luthi, B., and Furth, T. *The MeWe Generation.* Stockholm, Sweden: Bookhouse Publishing; 2005:67.
4. Kielburger, C. *Free the children.* New York: Harper Perennial; 1998. Kielburger, M., and Kielberger, C. *Take action! A guide to active citizenship.* Toronto, ON: Gage Learning; 2002.
5. Data available from the U.S. Bureau of Labor Statistics. Table 1: Volunteers by selected characteristics, September 2008. Economic News Release. Available at www.bls.gov/news.release/volun.t01.htm.
6. Schanberg, S. Convocation speech at the State University of New York at New Paltz. Available at www.chronogram.com/issue/2002/01/room2.htm. Accessed June 12, 2008.

Chapter 1

1. Dalai Lama, and McLeod, M. Educating the heart. *Shambhala Sun,* January 2006:61.

2. For more on these young people's stories of transitions during the decade after high school, see www.storiesoftranstion.org.

3. Staub, E. The psychology of perpetrators and bystanders. *Political Psychology;* 1985:6(1):61–85.

4. Milgrams, Stanley. *Obedience to authority: An experimental view.* New York: HarperCollins; 2004 (originally published 1974).

5. Piaget, J. *The moral judgement of the child.* New York: Free Press; 1965 (originally published 1932).

6. Nagin, D., and Tremblay, R.E. Trajectories of boys' physical aggression, opposition, and hyperactivity on the path to physically violent and nonviolent juvenile delinquency. *Child Development;* 1999:70:1181–96.

7. Clinton, B. *Giving: How each of us can change the world.* New York: Knopf; 2007.

Chapter 2

1. Stern, D.N. *The interpersonal world of the infant: A view from psychoanalysis and developmental psychology.* New York: Basic Books; 1985.

2. Marvin, R., Cooper, G., Hoffman, K., and Powell, B. The Circle of Security Project: Attachment-based intervention with caregiver-pre-school child dyads. *Attachment and Human Development;* 2002:4(1):107–24.

3. Mary Ainsworth, quoted in Karen, R. *Becoming attached: First relationships and how they shape our capacity to love.* New York: Oxford University Press; 1994:3.

Chapter 3

1. Kohut, H. Thoughts on narcissism and narcissistic rage. In P.H. Ornstein, ed., *Selected writings of Heinz Kohut: 1950–1978,* vol. 2. New York: Basic Books; 1978: 615–658.

2. Gordon, M. *The roots of empathy: Changing the world, child by child.* Toronto: Thomas Allen; 2006.

3. Gordon, M. Educating the heart (in conversation with Melvin McLeod). *Shambhala Sun,* January 2007: 64.

4. McKown, C., Weinstein, R.S. Teacher expectations, classroom context, and the achievement gap. *Journal of School Psychology;* 2008:46(3):235–61.

5. Greene, S.M., et al. Risk and resilience after divorce. In F. Walsh, ed., *Normal family processes,* 3rd ed. New York: Guilford; 2003:96–120.

Chapter 4

1. Benzaquén, A.S. *Encounters with wild children: Temptation and disappointment in the study of human nature.* Montreal: McGill-Queen's University Press; 2006:111.

2. Ibid., 245.

3. Statistics Canada. Time spent with children. *The Daily*; June 13, 2000. Available at www.statcan.ca/Daily/English/000613/d000613a.htm. Accessed May 4, 2007.

4. Lin, S. Attachment in cultural contexts: Ponderings and implications. *Family Therapy Magazine*; 2006:September/October: 28–32.

5. Good, E.P., Grumley, J., and Roy, S. *A connected school*. Chapel Hill, NC: New View Publications; 2003.

6. Ibid., 40–41.

7. Hammer, H., Finkelor, D., and Sedlak, A.J. Children abducted by family members: National estimates and characteristics. *National Incidence Studies of Missing, Abducted, Runaway, and Thrownaway Children*. Office of Juvenile Justice and Delinquency Prevention, U.S. Department of Justice; October 2002. Available at www.ojjdp.ncjrs.org. Accessed May 15, 2008.

8. Child Welfare Information Gateway. Child abuse and neglect fatalities: Statistics and interventions. Washington, DC: U.S. Department of Health and Human Services; March 2008. Trocme, N., et al. The Canadian Incidence Study of Reported Child Abuse and Neglect: Methodology and major findings. In K. Kufeldt and B. McKenzie, eds., *Child welfare: Connecting research, policy, and practice*. Waterloo, ON: Wilfrid Laurier Press; 2003:13–26.

9. Alaggia, R. Many ways of telling: expanding conceptualizations of child sexual abuse disclosure. *Child Abuse & Neglect*; 2004:28:1213–27. London, K., Bruck, M., Ceci, S.J., and Shuman, D.W. Disclosure of child sexual abuse: What does the research tell us about the ways that children tell? *Psychology, Public Policy and Law*; 2005:11(1):194–226.

10. Johnson, S. *Hold me tight: Seven conversations for a lifetime of love.* New York: Little, Brown and Company; 2008.

11. Wark, L. Look at me: What to tell parents about their young child's attachment. *Family Therapy Magazine*; 2006:September/October:12–16.

12. Ibid., 14.

13. Neill, A.S. *Summerhill: A radical approach to child rearing*. New York: Hart; 1960.

14. Dunphy, S. *Wednesday's child*. Dublin, Ireland: Gill & Mcmillan; 2006.

15. Lewis, S. *Race against time*. Toronto: House of Anasi Press; 2006: 35–36.

Chapter 5

1. Langille, D.B., Flowerdew, G., and Andreou, P. Teenage pregnancy in Nova Scotia communities: Associations with contextual factors. *Canadian Journal of Human Sexuality*; 2004:13(2):83–94. U.S. Centers for Disease Control and Prevention. Youth risk behavior surveillance: United States, 2005. *Morbidity and Mortality Weekly Report*; 2000:55(ss–5). Data Trends.

Available at www.childtrendsdatabank.org/indicators/23SexuallyActiveTeens
.cfm. Accessed February 11, 2007.

2. Nova Scotia Roundtable on Youth Sexual Health. *Framework for action: Youth sexual health.* Halifax, NS: Government of Nova Scotia; 2006.

3. See articles in van Voorhis, P., Braswell, M., and Lester, D. *Correctional counseling and rehabilitation,* 3rd ed. Cincinnati: Anderson Publishing; 1997. Williams, R. A. Multisystemic treatment of serious juvenile offenders: Long-term prevention of criminality and violence. *Journal of Consulting and Clinical Psychology;* 1995:63:569–78.

4. Chödrön, P. *Places that scare you.* Boston: Shambhala; 2002.

5. Peck, M.S. *The road less traveled.* New York: Touchstone; 2002.

6. Macy, J., and Brown, M.Y. *Coming back to life: Practices to reconnect our lives, our world.* Gabriola Island, BC: New Society; 1998.

7. Wackernagel, M., and Rees, W.E. *Our ecological footprint: Reducing human impact on the earth.* Gabriola Island, BC: New Society; 1996.

8. T.N. Hanh, quoted in McLeod, M. This is the Buddha's love. *Shambhala Sun,* March 2006:53.

Chapter 6

1. Dovidio, J.F., Piliavin, J.A., Schroeder, D.A., and Penner, L.A. *The social psychology of prosocial behavior.* Mahwah, NJ: Lawrence Erlbaum Associates; 2006:230.

2. Coloroso, B. *Extraordinary evil: A brief history of genocide.* Toronto: Penguin; 2007.

3. Dovidio, Piliarin, Schroeder, and Penner, *The social psychology.*

Chapter 7

1. De Botton, A. *The architecture of happiness.* New York: Vintage; 2006. Duany, A., Plater-Zyberk, E., and Speck, J. *Suburban nation: The rise of sprawl and the decline of the American dream.* New York: North Point Press; 2000.

2. Wente, M. Column. *Globe and Mail.* September 30: 2006: F6.

3. Turner, V. *The ritual process.* Chicago: Aldine; 1969.

4. A version of this story was previously published as Ungar, M. Family survival. *Toronto Star,* January 2005:1.

5. Schwartz, P. Peer marriage: How love between equals really works. New York: Maxwell MacMillan International; 1994.

6. McCubbin, L.D., and McCubbin, H.I. Culture and ethnic identity in family resilience: Dynamic processes in trauma and transformation of indigenous people. In M. Ungar, ed., *Handbook for working with children and youth: Pathways to resilience across cultures and contexts.* Thousand Oaks, CA: Sage; 2005:27–44.

7. Luthar, S. The culture of affluence: Psychological costs of material wealth. *Child Development*; 2003:74:1581–93:1582.

8. Barham, N. *Disconnected*. London: Random House; 2004.

9. Ibid., 306.

10. Ibid., 311.

Chapter 8

1. Bauman, Z. *Liquid modernity*. Cambridge, UK: Polity; 2000.

2. Jacobs, J. *The death and life of great American cities*. New York: Vintage; 1992.

3. Alexiou, A.S. *Jane Jacobs: Urban visionary*. Toronto: Harper; 2006:30.

4. Kennedy, C. Teens team up to give back. *Time* magazine; March 26, 2007:44.

5. Lalonde, C.E. Identity formation and cultural resilience in Aboriginal communities. In R.J. Flynn, P.M. Dudding, and J.G. Barber, eds., *Promoting resilience in child welfare*. Ottawa, ON: University of Ottawa Press; 2006:52–71.

6. Ibid., 67.

7. Putnam, R.D. *Making democracy work: Civic traditions in modern Italy*. Princeton, NJ: Princeton University Press; 1993. Putnam, R.D. *Bowling alone: The collapse of American community*. New York: Simon & Schuster; 2000.

8. Adapted from Benson, P. L. *All kids are our kids*. Minneapolis: Search Institute; 1997.

9. Ibid., 11.

10. Kielburger, M., and Kielburger, C. *Take action! A guide to active citizenship*. Toronto, ON: Gage Learning; 2002:vii.

Conclusion

1. America by the numbers: What we buy. *Time* magazine. Available at www.time.com/time/magazine/article/20061030_what_we_buy.pdf. Accessed June 10, 2007.

2. Perkins, D.F., et al. Participation in structured youth programs: Why ethnic minority urban youth choose to participate—or not to participate. *Youth and Society*; 2007:38:420–42.

3. Winnicott, D.W. *The maturational process and the facilitating environment*. New York: International Universities Press; 1965.

INDEX